# *Food for*
# BABIES
# & Toddlers

First published in 2014 by Bauer Media Books, Australia. Reprinted in 2014.
Bauer Media Books are published by Bauer Media Pty Limited.

MEDIA GROUP

## BAUER MEDIA BOOKS

**Publisher** Jo Runciman
**Editorial & food director** Pamela Clark
**Director of sales, marketing & rights** Brian Cearnes
**Creative director** Hieu Chi Nguyen
**Art director & designer** Hannah Blackmore
**Food editor** Emma Braz
**Senior business analyst** Rebecca Varela
**Operations manager** David Scotto
**Production controller** Corinne Whitsun-Jones

Published by Bauer Media Books,
a division of Bauer Media Ltd,
54 Park St, Sydney; GPO Box 4088,
Sydney, NSW 2001, Australia
phone (02) 9282 8618; fax (02) 9267 9438
www.awwcookbooks.com.au

**Cover photographer** Louise Lister
**Cover stylist** Louise Bickle
**Cover photochef** Sharon Kennedy
**Additional photography** Louise Lister
**Additional styling** Louise Bickle
**Photochef** Sharon Kennedy

**Printed in** China with 1010 Printing Asia Limited.
**Australia** Distributed by Network Services,
phone +61 2 9282 8777; fax +61 2 9264 3278;
networkweb@networkservicescompany.com.au
**New Zealand** Distributed by Bookreps NZ Ltd,
phone +64 9 419 2635; fax +64 9 419 2634;
susan@bookreps.co.nz
**South Africa** Distributed by PSD Promotions,
phone +27 11 392 6065/6/7; fax +27 11 392 6079/80;
orders@psdprom.co.za  www.psdpromotions.com

Title: Food for babies & toddlers / food director, Pamela Clark.
ISBN: 978 174245 481 8 (paperback)
Notes: Includes index.
Subjects: Cooking (Baby foods) Baby foods.
Other Authors/Contributors: Clark, Pamela, editor.
Dewey Number: 641.56222

© Bauer Media Pty Limited 2014
ABN 18 053 273 546

The publishers would like to thank the following for props used in photography:
Lifefactory: www.until.com.au/stockists;
Paper 2: www.paper2.com.au;
KIDO: www.kidostore.com

**To order books**
**phone** 136 116 (within Australia) or
**order online** at www.awwcookbooks.com.au
Send recipe enquiries to:
recipeenquiries@bauer-media.com.au

THE AUSTRALIAN

# Women's Weekly

# Food for
# BABIES
# & Toddlers

BAUER
MEDIA GROUP

# contents

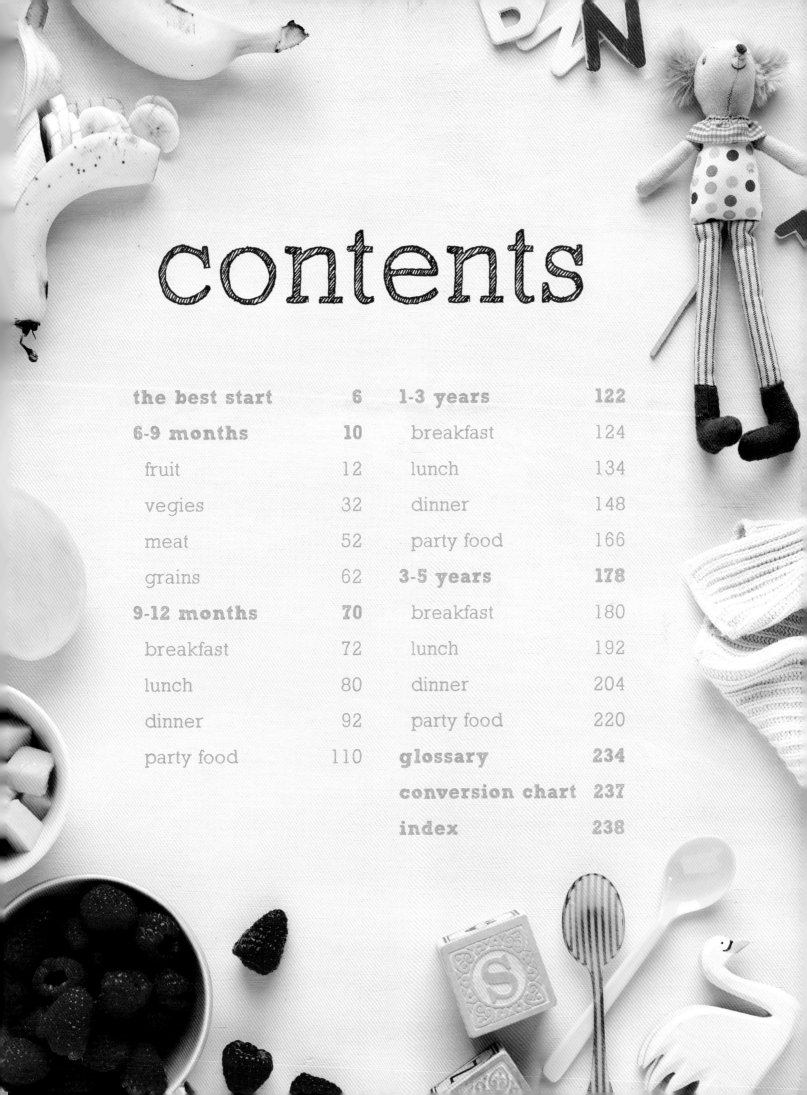

# the best start

Having a baby is the ultimate responsibility. As a dietitian and health educator, I love working with parents of babies and young children. There are few other times in life when I find someone more motivated and inspired to set good eating habits in place. This little person relies on you to give them everything they need – and that includes their nutrition.

## Nutrition in the first years of life

From the time a baby is born to when they start school, their rate of growth and development is enormous. In the first six months most babies double their birth weight. In the second half of the first year, growth is not quite so rapid, and from there children tend to gain on average 2.5kg a year until the age of five. To put this in perspective, an average 3kg baby at birth grows to be an 18kg, 5 year old. But they will only grow to their genetic potential with the right nutrition.

Growth requires protein to build new cells for tissue, bones, blood, brain cells and so on. A wide range of vitamins and minerals are required for these processes. B-group vitamins are essential to convert food into energy to fuel their growing bodies. Various minerals including calcium and phosphorus are required for bone growth. Iron is required to form healthy blood cells that are able to carry oxygen and nutrients around the body. Omega-3 fats are required for optimal brain development. Vitamin A plays a crucial role in the development of the eyes. The thyroid gland needs iodine, and without adequate iodine growth is stunted. And so on. All of these nutrients are found in foods and, as guardians of young children, we need to ensure the right balance of foods are made available to them.

## Breast is best

In Australia, the Infant Feeding Guidelines were renewed and updated in 2013. Research has shown breastfeeding, without doubt, is the best way to feed your baby. The new guidelines recommend you exclusively breastfeed your baby to around 6 months of age, which is the optimal time to start to introduce solids. Provided you and the baby are happy and willing to do so, it is recommended you continue to breastfeed until 12 months, and for longer if you so choose. However this doesn't suit every mother, and it's important to take all factors into account.

The bottom line is that any breastfeeding is enormously beneficial to your baby. One of the benefits of breastfeeding is that it provides exactly the right nutrients and in a form that is best absorbed by your baby. And, importantly, breastfeeding helps provide immunity against infections and diseases. Research has shown that breastfeeding to around 6 months reduces the risk of obesity, diabetes and cardiovascular (heart) disease later in life; this really illustrates that how we feed our children early in life has a lifelong impact on their health.

## Introducing solid food

The latest guidelines, based on current research, recommend that you introduce solids at around

6 months. The reason for this is primarily two fold. Firstly, by this age infants need more iron than can be supplied by breast milk alone; and secondly, exclusive breastfeeding to around 6 months significantly reduces the risk of your baby developing allergies. If you start solids too early, or delay much longer than 6 months, the risk of allergies is actually increased. Of course, every baby is different; be guided by your baby and speak with your health-care professional if you are unsure.

## Which foods are best?

There is no definitive guide for which foods you should introduce first, nor do you need to stick to the now out-of-date advice to wait a few days before introducing a new food. You can choose the order and rate at which you introduce new foods, provided you follow some basic guidelines.

• **Texture is important**; during the first stage foods should be smooth. Start by puréeing foods and after a month or so gradually move towards mashing. By 9 months your baby should be managing lumpy foods with some texture. By this stage you can simply mash foods with a fork.

• **Whole nuts and other hard foods are a choking hazard**, but many parents are unaware that they should not be introduced until after age 3; this includes popcorn. You can give your baby smooth nut butters; in fact these are great foods to include as they are rich in healthy fats, fibre, plant protein, magnesium and many other essential nutrients.

• **Do not add any salt** to your baby's food. I'm all for giving your baby family meals as early as possible – it makes life much easier for you and it gets the baby accustomed to a variety of tastes right from the start. So be sure to cook without any added salt so you are able to purée a portion for your baby.

• **Do not add any sugar** to foods. Babies have an innate likeness for sweet, but by adding sugar you are simply giving them kilojoules without any additional nutrients. Honey has a tiny, but nevertheless present, risk of carrying the bacteria that causes botulism. Honey is not recommended until after 12 months of age.

• **Include iron-rich foods**. Iron is a key nutrient required at this stage. There are two types of iron – haem iron in animal foods including meat, fish and poultry, and non-haem iron found in plant foods such as legumes, tofu and leafy greens such as spinach. Haem iron is absorbed four times better than non-haem iron.

You can also use iron-fortified baby cereals, although be aware these can cause constipation in some babies. Personally, I'm not a fan of baby rice cereal, as it's essentially a highly-processed food and has an extremely high glycaemic index (GI). Such foods were not available until relatively recently, so they are certainly not necessary for your baby. I favour buying fresh whole foods and processing them yourself to the required consistency.

## Reducing the risk of allergies

One important change in recent guidelines is with regards to potentially allergenic foods, such as peanuts, egg, cow's milk and fish. The Australasian Society of Clinical Immunology and Allergy states that delaying the introduction of these foods does not reduce the risk of food allergies or eczema – even if you have an older child with an existing allergy. There is some suggestion that avoiding such foods during pregnancy, breastfeeding and in infant life, actually increases the likelihood of an allergy. Until we understand more about what causes food allergies to develop, the advice is to include these foods as appropriate.

What we do know is that babies exclusively breastfed for 6 months have a significantly reduced risk of allergic rhinitis, wheezing, asthma and atopy (a predisposition towards allergies). More recent studies have shown that continuing to breastfeed while potentially allergenic foods are introduced may offer some protection. So if you can, keep breastfeeding while introducing these foods.

## Moving to finger foods

Once your baby is around 9 months they develop much better hand control and will likely want to start feeding themselves. Encourage this by letting them have a go at holding their spoon and giving them easy to eat, soft finger foods. Avoid hard foods such as apple, raw carrot or celery as these will be difficult for your baby to chew and may cause them to choke. You can lightly steam or microwave carrot sticks to make them suitable. Stay with them while they are eating and ensure they sit in their high chair rather than wandering around – otherwise they risk choking or become distracted and not focus on the task at hand.

## Feeding your toddler

Your baby's first birthday is a major landmark, and a few things change from a nutritional perspective. You can now give regular full-fat cow's milk – special toddler milk formulas are not necessary. Be sure to ditch the bottles if you have not already done so, and switch to a sippy cup instead.

Honey is now safe to eat, so you can drizzle it on porridge for breakfast, or serve it with nut butter on toast as a nutritious snack.

Your toddler should be joining in family meals. While they may not be ready to tuck into steak and salad, most meals can be adapted to suit everyone around the table. Bear in mind that young children have small stomachs, so can't go as long between meals as adults. They will need to eat smaller more regular meals. This doesn't mean eating food all day long – this only results in your child never being properly hungry, nor truly satisfied. You have no chance of them devouring your wholesome homemade dinner if they've been grazing on bits and pieces all afternoon. Encourage a schedule – for most children, 3 meals and 3 snacks will suffice – and discourage eating outside of this.

During mealtimes offer only water. Children can become 'milkaholics' if they are allowed to fall back to drinking bottles of milk instead of eating. As a concerned parent you might be thinking it's better to get something into them but, rest assured, your child will not starve. Keep in mind your job is to provide nutritious food, and your toddler can decide how much of it they eat. Trust that at this age children are very good at eating the amount they require, provided the right foods are on offer.

Make water the drink of choice. Offer milk as part of a snack, but avoid offering it all day long. Fruit juice can easily be over-consumed and, while it's okay on occasion, it is much better to get your child eating whole fruit and drinking water. Soft drinks are not suitable.

Bear in mind that fruit juices and soft drinks, be they sugar-free or regular, are all acidic and damaging to tooth enamel. For the healthy development of your child's teeth, it is best to avoid these drinks altogether.

# Dealing with a fussy eater

Toddlers can be fussy, and that's a normal part of development. They learn that they have some control in their lives and choosing to eat or not eat certain foods is one of those things. It is crucial that you deal with this in the right way from the start. It's much harder to change ingrained behaviours at a later stage.

One of the best strategies is to give them some choice – but make that choice between a couple of healthy options. Ask if they would like carrot or broccoli with dinner, boiled eggs or porridge for breakfast, tuna or cold meat in their sandwich, and so on.

Take them shopping when you are not rushed, and use it as an opportunity to teach them about foods; let them help with things like fruit and vegetable selections. Let them 'help' in the kitchen so they feel they have played a role in the meal. Not only does this start teaching them about food and nutrition, they'll be far more interested in the meal and more likely to eat it.

Don't let mealtimes become a battleground. If they won't eat, tell them this is all that is on offer and they can choose not to eat, but there will be nothing else until next mealtime. Even if this results in tears, tantrums and going to bed hungry, your child will not waste away before the next meal. Stick to your guns and in all likelihood you'll find that dinner goes down much more easily. The worst thing you can do is to give in and give them whatever the easy favourite is. They will soon learn that if they make enough of a fuss, they get what they want. You'll be setting yourself up for many months, and potentially years, of problems.

Young children have more sensitive taste buds than adults, so vegies like cabbage and broccoli can taste more bitter to them. They also have an innate aversion to try new foods. Research has shown that it can actually take 15 or more exposures to a new food before a child will accept it. So don't give up – without making a fuss, put a little on their plate on a regular basis and eventually they just might take to it and like it. You can also try serving it up in different ways, and it does help to introduce new foods alongside a more familiar dish. An entirely new meal might be overwhelming to a toddler.

Finally, don't assume children won't like a food. Time and time again I hear parents in restaurants telling their kids 'oh you won't like that'. If you make that assumption you'll be forever ordering from those dreadful kids' menus. Encourage them to taste and discuss various foods. Let them see you enjoying a variety of foods and make mealtimes pleasurable. These aspects of eating are just as important as the nutritional qualities of the meal.

Dr Joanna McMillan
**Accredited Practising Dietitian and Nutritionist**
**www.drjoanna.com.au**
**www.getlean.com.au**

# 6-9 months

This is the exciting stage of introducing your baby to solid foods. If you are willing and able, continuing to breastfeed during this transition will benefit both you and your baby. The goal over this three-month period is to increase the variety of foods your baby eats, ensure they obtain all of the nutrients they require – paying particular attention to iron – and move them gradually from puréed silky smooth foods, to foods with a mushy lumpy consistency. This is important to help them to develop the muscles they need for chewing and speech.

# FRUIT

Use unblemished and undamaged, fresh in-season fruit (or vegetables); this way you'll know your baby is getting top-quality vitamins and minerals. To prevent cross contamination, prepare them on a cutting board used just for fruit (you should have a number of different cutting boards, each dedicated to one type of food, eg fruit, vegetables, meat, dairy, seafood). All equipment, including your hands and tea towels, should be clean. Don't use kitchen sponges to wash equipment or wipe down cutting boards, as these are difficult to keep clean and are notorious for harbouring bacteria.

## apple purée

suitable from 6 months

Combine 2 large peeled, cored and coarsely chopped apples and 2 tablespoons of water in a medium saucepan; bring to the boil over medium heat. Reduce heat to low; simmer, uncovered, for 10 minutes or until tender. Cool slightly; blend or process apple mixture until smooth. Give your child as much fruit purée as desired.

**prep + cook time** 15 minutes (+ cooling)
**makes** 1 cup (12 tablespoons)
**tips** Store, covered, in the fridge for up to 1 day. Purée is suitable to freeze, in 1-tablespoon portions in ice-cube trays, covered, for up to 1 month.

## banana purée

suitable from 6 months

Blend or process 2 medium coarsely chopped bananas until smooth. Give your child as much fruit purée as desired.

**prep time** 5 minutes  **makes** 1 cup (12 tablespoons)
**tips** This starts to discolour fairly quickly, so spoon out only as much as needed, and freeze the rest immediately. Purée is suitable to freeze, in 1-tablespoon portions in ice-cube trays, covered, for up to 1 month.

# pear purée

**suitable from 6 months**

Combine 1 large peeled, cored, coarsely chopped pear and 2 tablespoons of water in a medium saucepan; bring to the boil. Reduce heat; simmer, uncovered, for 20 minutes or until tender. Cool slightly; blend or process pear mixture until smooth. Give your child as much fruit purée as desired.

**prep + cook time** 25 minutes (+ cooling)
**makes** 1 cup (12 tablespoons)
**tips** Store, covered, in the fridge for up to 1 day. Purée is suitable to freeze, in 1-tablespoon portions in ice-cube trays, covered, for up to 1 month.

# apple and prune mash

**suitable from 6 months**

Combine 2 large peeled, cored, thinly sliced apples, ⅓ cup thinly sliced, seeded prunes and ¼ cup of water in a medium saucepan; bring to the boil. Reduce heat to low; simmer, covered, until apple and prune are tender. Cool slightly; blend, process or mash apple mixture until the desired consistency is reached. Give your child as much fruit mash as desired.

**prep + cook time** 20 minutes (+ cooling)
**makes** 1 cup (12 tablespoons)
**tips** Store, covered, in the fridge for up to 1 day. Fruit mash is suitable to freeze, in 1-tablespoon portions in ice-cube trays, covered, for up to 1 month.

# apricot mash

**suitable from 6 months**

Drain 425g (13½ ounces) canned apricots in natural juice over a large jug; reserve liquid. Blend, process or mash apricots with enough of the reserved liquid until you get the desired consistency. Give your child as much fruit mash as desired.

**prep time** 5 minutes  **makes** 1 cup (12 tablespoons)
**tips**  Store, covered, in the fridge for up to 1 day. Apricot mash is suitable to freeze, in 1-tablespoon portions in ice-cube trays, covered, for up to 1 month.

# blueberry purée

**suitable from 6 months**

Combine 300g (9½ ounces) coarsely chopped blueberries and 2 tablespoons of water in a medium saucepan; bring to the boil over medium heat. Reduce heat to low; simmer, uncovered, for 5 minutes or until softened. Cool slightly; push blueberries through a sieve into a small bowl. Give your child as much blueberry purée as desired.

**prep + cook time** 10 minutes (+ cooling)
**makes** 1 cup (12 tablespoons)
**tips**  Store, covered, in the fridge for up to 1 day. Blueberry purée is suitable to freeze, in 1-tablespoon portions in ice-cube trays, covered, for up to 1 month.

# rockmelon purée

Blend or process 500g (1 pound) peeled (all green sections removed) seeded and coarsely chopped rockmelon until smooth. Give your child as much fruit purée as desired.

**prep time** 5 minutes  **makes** 1 cup (12 tablespoons)
**tips**  Store, covered, in the fridge for up to 1 day. Purée is suitable to freeze, in 1-tablespoon portions in ice-cube trays, covered, for up to 1 month.

# custard apple purée

**suitable from 6 months**

Blend or process 400g (12½ ounces) peeled, seeded and coarsely chopped custard apple until smooth. Give your child as much fruit purée as desired.

**prep time** 10 minutes
**makes** 1 cup (12 tablespoons)
**tips** Store, covered, in the fridge for up to 1 day. Purée is suitable to freeze, in 1-tablespoon portions in ice-cube trays, covered, for up to 1 month.

# avocado purée

**suitable from 6 months**

Blend or process 2 small peeled, seeded and coarsely chopped avocadoes until smooth. Give your child as much fruit purée as desired.

**prep time** 5 minutes
**makes** 1 cup (12 tablespoons)
**tips** Avocado is best served at the time of making. The purée is suitable to freeze, in 1-tablespoon batches in ice-cube trays, covered, for up to 1 month.

## grape mash

**suitable from 6 months**

Blend, process or mash 250g (8 ounces) coarsely chopped seedless grapes until you get the desired consistency; you may need to add a little water, if needed. Give your child as much grape mash as desired.

**prep time** 5 minutes  **makes** 1 cup (12 tablespoons)
**tips**  Store, covered, in the fridge for up to 1 day. Grape mash is suitable to freeze, in 1-tablespoon portions in ice-cube trays, covered, for up to 1 month.

## mandarin mash

**suitable from 6 months**

Peel and discard pith and seeds from 2 medium mandarins. Blend, process or mash mandarin flesh with 1 tablespoon of apple juice until the desired consistency is reached. Give your child as much mandarin mash as desired.

**prep time** 10 minutes  **makes** 1 cup (12 tablespoons)
**tips**  Store, covered, in the fridge for up to 1 day. Mandarin mash is suitable to freeze, in 1-tablespoon portions in ice-cube trays, covered, for up to 1 month.

## mango mash

**suitable from 6 months**

Blend, process or mash 2 small peeled, seeded and coarsely chopped mangoes until the desired consistency is reached (add a little water, if needed). Give your child as much mango mash as desired.

**prep time** 10 minutes  **makes** 1 cup (12 tablespoons)
**tips**  Store, covered, in the fridge for up to 1 day. Mango mash is suitable to freeze, in 1-tablespoon portions in ice-cube trays, covered, for up to 1 month.

## papaya mash

**suitable from 6 months**

Blend, process or mash 1 small peeled, seeded and coarsely chopped papaya until desired consistency is reached (add a little water, if needed). Give your child as much papaya mash as desired.

**prep time** 10 minutes  **makes** 1 cup (12 tablespoons)
**tips**  Store, covered, in the fridge for up to 1 day. Papaya mash is suitable to freeze, in 1-tablespoon portions in ice-cube trays, covered, for up to 1 month.

# banana and egg yolk custard

suitable from 8 months

Bring ⅔ cup breast milk or formula, a pinch of cinnamon and ¼ teaspoon vanilla extract to the boil in a small saucepan; remove from heat. Whisk 1 egg yolk, ¼ of a ripe mashed banana and 1 teaspoon cornflour in a small bowl until combined. Pour milk mixture over banana mixture, whisking continuously until combined. Return mixture to pan; cook, stirring over low heat, until mixture just boils and thickens. Remove from heat; cover surface of custard with plastic wrap. Cool to room temperature. Give your child as much custard as desired.

**prep + cook time** 15 minutes (+ cooling)
**makes** ¾ cup (9 tablespoons)
**tips** The custard is best eaten close to serving. Recipe is not suitable to freeze.

# ricotta with pear purée

suitable from 8 months

Process ½ medium peeled, cored and halved ripe pear in the small bowl of a food processor until smooth. Add ⅔ cup ricotta and process again until smooth. Add a little breast milk or cooled boiled water if necessary to thin.

**prep time** 10 minutes  **makes** ⅔ cup (8 tablespoons)
**tips** Store, covered, in the fridge for up to 1 day. Recipe is not suitable to freeze.

## apple semolina

suitable from 6 months

Combine 3 teaspoons fine semolina, ⅓ cup of cooled boiled water and ⅓ cup apple juice in a small saucepan; simmer over medium heat, uncovered, for 2 minutes or until thickened. Cool slightly; stir in a little breast milk if desired, or for older babies, yoghurt. Give your child as much apple semolina as desired.

**prep + cook time** 10 minutes (+ cooling) **makes** ⅔ cup (8 tablespoons)
**tips** Store semolina, covered, in the refrigerator for up to 2 days. Recipe is not suitable to freeze.

## apricot purée with blended rice cereal

suitable from 6 months

Combine ⅔ cup dried apricots and 1¼ cups of water in a small saucepan; simmer, covered, over medium heat for 20 minutes, or until apricots are tender. Blend or process apricots and the cooking water until smooth. Mix 2 tablespoons blended rice cereal in a small bowl with 4 tablespoons of breast milk; serve topped with 1-2 tablespoons of the apricot purée. Cool slightly. Give your child as much purée as desired.

**prep + cook time** 25 minutes (+ cooling)
**makes** 1¼ cups (15 tablespoons)
**tip** Store purée, covered, in the fridge for up to 2 days. Purée is suitable to freeze in 1-tablespoon batches in ice-cube trays, covered, for up to 1 month.

# peach and apricot purée

**suitable from 6 months**

Combine 2 tablespoons apricot mash (see page 15) with 2 tablespoons peach mash (see page 24).

**prep time** 5 minutes **makes** ⅓ cup (4 tablespoons)

**tip** Make the peach and apricot mashes, store in the freezer in 1-tablespoon lots. Reheat frozen portions in a microwave oven on MEDIUM (50%) power until just warmed; mix together just before serving.

# apple and avocado purée

**suitable from 6 months**

Combine 2 tablespoons apple purée (see page 13) with 1 tablespoon avocado purée (see page 17).

**prep time** 5 minutes  **makes** ¼ cup (3 tablespoons)

**tip**  Make the apple and avocado purées, store in the freezer in 1-tablespoon lots. Reheat frozen portions in a microwave oven on MEDIUM (50%) power until just warmed; mix together just before serving.

# apple and blueberry purée

**suitable from 6 months**

Combine 2 large peeled, cored and coarsely chopped red apples, ½ cup frozen blueberries and 1 tablespoon of water in a small saucepan; bring to the boil. Reduce heat to low; simmer, covered, about 10 minutes or until fruit is tender.  Cool slightly; blend mixture until smooth. Push purée through a sieve to remove any pieces of skin.

**prep + cook time** 20 minutes (+ cooling)

**makes** 1 cup (12 tablespoons)

**tips**  We used red apples in the apple and blueberry purée as green apples are often too tart for infants. Golden delicious apples can be used (for both apple recipes), as they are quite sweet. Store, covered, in the fridge for up to 1 day. The purée is suitable to freeze, in 1-tablespoon portions in ice-cube trays, covered, for up to 1 month.

# apple and rice cereal

suitable from 6 months

Blend 3 tablespoons baby rice cereal with 1 cup of water in
a small saucepan; stir over medium heat until mixture boils
and thickens. Cool to room temperature. Make apple purée
(see page 13); cool. Combine 1 tablespoon of rice cereal with
1 tablespoon of apple purée to serve.

**prep + cook time** 15 minutes (+ cooling)
**makes** 2 cups (24 tablespoons)
**tip** This recipe makes 1 cup rice cereal purée and 1 cup apple
purée. Store, separately, covered, in the fridge for up to 1 day.
Freeze the purées separately in 1-tablespoon batches in
ice-cube trays, covered, for up to 1 month. Reheat 1 frozen
portion each in a microwave oven on MEDIUM (50%) power
until just warmed; mix together just before serving. Add rice
cereal to other fruit purées, if you like.

# peach mash

suitable from 6 months

Blend, process or mash 425g (13½ ounces) drained canned
peaches in natural juice until the desired consistency is
reached (add a little of the drained juice, if needed). Give
your child as much fruit mash as desired.

**prep time** 5 minutes  **makes** 1 cup (12 tablespoons)
**tips** Store, covered, in the fridge for up to 1 day. Purée is
suitable to freeze, in 1-tablespoon portions in ice-cube trays,
covered, for up to 1 month.

# banana and rockmelon purée

suitable from 6 months

Push 1 tablespoon passionfruit pulp through a sieve over a small bowl; discard seeds. Blend or process 100g (3 ounces) coarsely chopped ripe rockmelon and ½ medium coarsely chopped ripe banana with passionfruit juice until smooth.

**prep time** 10 minutes  **makes** ⅔ cup (8 tablespoons)
**tips**  You will need 2 passionfruit for the banana and rockmelon purée. This recipe is not suitable to freeze.

# peach and raspberry purée

suitable from 6 months

Preheat oven to 180°C/350°F. Place 2 medium halved, ripe peaches, cut-side down, in an ovenproof dish; add ¼ cup of water. Roast for 15 minutes or until peaches are tender; cool. Discard skin. Blend or process peaches with 125g (4 ounces) fresh or frozen raspberries until smooth. Push mixture through a sieve into a small bowl.

**prep + cook time** 25 minutes (+ cooling)
**makes** 1 cup (12 tablespoons)
**tips**  Use ripe peaches for this purée as under-ripe fruit will give a sour-tasting purée. Store, covered, in the fridge for up to 1 day. Purée is suitable to freeze, in 1-tablespoon portions in ice-cube trays, covered, for up to 1 month.

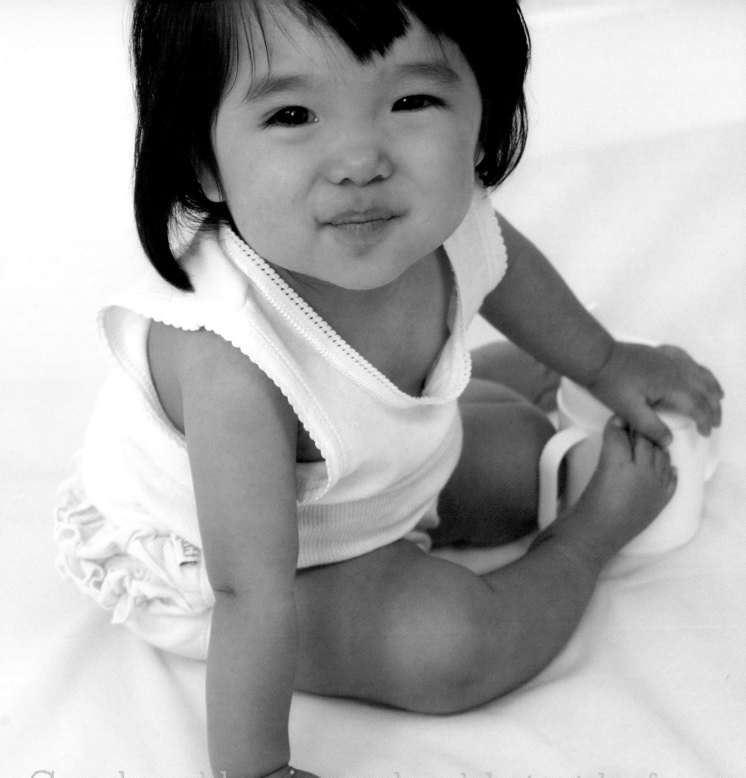

Good oral hygiene should start before teeth even appear by gently wiping gums with a clean damp cloth. Teeth begin to emerge from 3½ to 16 months; use a baby's toothbrush and brush only with water for the first 18 months.

# banana with semolina

suitable from 6 months

Blend 2 teaspoons fine semolina and ⅓ cup of water in a small saucepan; stir over medium heat until mixture boils and thickens. Cool to room temperature. Push 1 small overripe banana through a sieve into a small bowl. Combine 1 tablespoon semolina with 1 tablespoon banana purée to serve. Give your child as much semolina as desired.

**prep + cook time** 15 minutes (+ cooling)
**makes** ⅓ cup semolina; 2½ tablespoons banana purée
**tips** Store semolina, covered, in the fridge for up to 1 day. The purée is best eaten on the day of making. Recipe is not suitable to freeze.

# pear and date purée

suitable from 6 months

Combine 2 medium peeled coarsely chopped pears, 3 fresh seeded coarsely chopped dates and ¼ cup of water in a small saucepan; bring to the boil. Reduce heat to low; simmer, covered, for 10 minutes or until fruit is tender. Cool slightly; blend or process mixture until smooth. Push mixture through a sieve into a small bowl. Give your child as much purée as desired.

**prep + cook time** 20 minutes (+ cooling)
**makes** 1 cup (12 tablespoons)
**tip** Store, covered, in the fridge for up to 1 day. Purée is suitable to freeze, in 1-tablespoon portions in ice-cube trays, covered, for up to 1 month.

# roasted apples, plums and vanilla mash

Preheat oven to 200°C/400°F. Line a small oven tray with baking paper. Cut 2 large peeled, cored, red apples into eighths. Halve and remove stone from 1 medium plum. Place fruit close together on the tray. Sprinkle with 3 teaspoons of water. Roast for 20 minutes or until tender. Transfer fruit to a small bowl, add ¼ teaspoon vanilla extract. Mash with a fork to desired consistency. Cool slightly. Give your child as much mash as desired.

**prep + cook time** 30 minutes (+ cooling)
**makes** ¾ cup (9 tablespoons)
**tips** Store, covered, in the fridge for up to 2 days. Purée is suitable to freeze, in 1-tablespoon portions in ice-cube trays, covered, for up to 1 month. You can use many other fruits for this recipe, such as nectarines, apricots, peaches and pears.

# rhubarb, apple and yoghurt purée

**suitable from 6 months**

Combine 1 cup (110g) coarsely chopped fresh or frozen rhubarb, 1 medium peeled, cored and finely chopped apple, a pinch of cinnamon (optional) and ¼ cup water in a small saucepan; bring to the boil over medium heat. Reduce heat to low; simmer, uncovered, stirring occasionally, for 10 minutes or until rhubarb is tender. Transfer to a medium heatproof bowl. Cover; refrigerate for 1 hour. Blend or process rhubarb mixture with ⅔ cup (190g) vanilla yoghurt until smooth.

**prep + cook time** 20 minutes (+ cooling)
**makes** 2 cups (24 tablespoons)
**tips** Store, covered, in the fridge for up to 1 day. Purée is suitable to freeze in individual portions without yoghurt; freeze, in 1-tablespoon portions in ice-cube trays, covered, for up to 1 month. Purée fruit and swirl it through the yoghurt, if you like.

## apple yoghurt with cinnamon

**suitable from 8 months**

Peel and coarsely grate ½ small fresh apple; using a sharp knife, chop the grated apple until finely chopped. Finely chop 1 tablespoon sultanas. Combine the apple and sultanas with ⅓ cup yoghurt and a tiny pinch ground cinnamon in a small bowl. Sprinkle with a little extra ground cinnamon, if you like. Give your child as much yoghurt as desired.

**prep time** 5 minutes  **makes** ½ cup (6 tablespoons)
**tips**  Store, covered, in the fridge for up to 2 days. Recipe is not suitable to freeze.

## mango and passionfruit yoghurt

**suitable from 6 months**

Blend or process ½ cup yoghurt and ¼ small coarsely chopped ripe mango until smooth. Strain 1 passionfruit; discard seeds. Drizzle yoghurt with 2 teaspoons strained passionfruit pulp. Give your child as much yoghurt as desired.

**prep time** 5 minutes  **makes** ⅔ cup (8 tablespoons)
**tips**  Store, covered, in the fridge for up to 2 days. This recipe is not suitable to freeze.

# raspberry and pear yoghurt

suitable from 6 months

Melt 10g (½ ounce) butter in a small saucepan over medium heat. Add 1 medium peeled, cored, thinly sliced ripe pear and 125g (4 ounces) fresh or frozen raspberries; cook, stirring occasionally, for 10 minutes or until pear is tender. Cool; blend until smooth. Transfer to a small bowl, fold through ¾ cup vanilla yoghurt. Give your child as much yoghurt as desired.

**prep + cook time** 15 minutes (+ cooling)
**makes** ¾ cup (9 tablespoons)
**tips**  Store, covered, in the fridge for up to 2 days. Recipe is not suitable to freeze. You can use other fruits, such as apple, plum, banana, blueberries and nectarines.

# VEGIES

Iron is an important mineral for growing babies. Plant sources of iron include tofu (from compressed crushed soya beans), leafy green vegetables, such as spinach, and legumes (beans, lentils and chickpeas). Including a vitamin C rich food in the same meal will help your baby absorb the iron from plant sources. For example, combine puréed canned beans with spinach and the juice from a freshly squeezed orange. This is especially important if you wish to raise your child on a vegetarian diet. See page 12 for tips on preventing cross contamination.

# broccoli purée

suitable from 6 months

Coarsely chop the stems of 250g (8 ounces) broccoli, cut remaining broccoli into florets. Steam broccoli stems and florets until tender; drain. Cool slightly; blend or process broccoli until smooth, add up to 2 tablespoons of breast milk or cooled boiled water. Give your child as much broccoli purée as desired.

**prep + cook time** 15 minutes (+ cooling)
**makes** 1 cup (12 tablespoons)
**tips** Store, covered, in the fridge for up to 2 days. Purée is suitable to freeze, in 1-tablespoon portions in ice-cube trays, covered, for up to 1 month.

# carrot purée

suitable from 6 months

Peel and coarsely chop 2 large carrots. Steam carrots for 15 minutes or until tender; drain. Cool slightly; blend or process carrot with 2 tablespoons of breast milk or cooled boiled water until smooth. Give your child as much carrot purée as desired.

**prep + cook time** 20 minutes (+ cooling)
**makes** 1 cup (12 tablespoons)
**tips** Store, covered, in the fridge for up to 2 days. Purée is suitable to freeze, in 1-tablespoon portions in ice-cube trays, covered, for up to 1 month.

# spinach purée

suitable from 6 months

Trim and discard stems then coarsely chop 250g (8 ounces) spinach. Steam spinach for 8 minutes or until tender; drain. Cool slightly; blend or process spinach with approximately 1 tablespoon breast milk or cooled boiled water until smooth. Give your child as much spinach purée as desired.

**prep + cook time** 15 minutes (+ cooling)
**makes** 1 cup (12 tablespoons)
**tips** Store, covered, in the fridge for up to 2 days. Purée is suitable to freeze, in 1-tablespoon portions in ice-cube trays, covered, for up to 1 month.

# asparagus mash

suitable from 6 months

Trim and coarsely chop 300g (9½ ounces) asparagus. Steam asparagus for 5 minutes or until tender; drain. Cool slightly; blend, process or mash asparagus with a little breast milk or cooled boiled water, if needed, until the desired consistency is reached. Give your child as much asparagus mash as desired.

**prep + cook time** 5 minutes (+ cooling)
**makes** 1 cup (12 tablespoons)
**tips** Store, covered, in the fridge for up to 2 days. Asparagus mash is suitable to freeze, in 1-tablespoon portions in ice-cube trays, covered, for up to 1 month.

# button mushroom mash

suitable from 6 months

Finely chop 300g (9½ ounces) button mushrooms. Melt 20g (¾ ounce) butter in a medium frying pan; cook mushrooms, stirring, until tender. Cool slightly; blend, process or mash mushrooms until the desired consistency is reached. Give your child as much mash as desired.

**prep + cook time** 10 minutes (+ cooling)
**makes** 1 cup (12 tablespoons)
**tips** Store, covered, in the fridge for up to 1 day. Purée is suitable to freeze, in 1-tablespoon portions in ice-cube trays, covered, for up to 1 month.

# bean mash

suitable from 6 months

Trim and coarsely chop 300g (9½ ounces) green beans. Steam beans for 10 minutes or until tender; drain. Cool slightly; blend, process or mash beans with a little breast milk or cooled boiled water, if needed, until the desired consistency is reached. Give your child as much bean mash as desired.

**prep + cook time** 15 minutes (+ cooling)
**makes** 1 cup (12 tablespoons)
**tips** Store, covered, in the fridge for up to 1 day. Purée is suitable to freeze, in 1-tablespoon portions in ice-cube trays, covered, for up to 1 month.

## potato and spinach purée

suitable from 6 months

Combine 2 tablespoons potato purée (see page 39) with 1 tablespoon spinach purée (see page 34). Give your child as much purée as desired.

**prep + cook time** 5 minutes  **makes** ¼ cup (3 tablespoons)
**tips**  Reheat single frozen portions of puréed potato and spinach in a microwave oven on MEDIUM (50%) power until just warm, then combine them just before serving. You could also make this purée combination while cooking the individual purées; freeze in 1-tablespoon batches in ice-cube trays, covered, for up to 1 month.

## vegetable and cheese mash

suitable from 6 months

Combine 1 tablespoon asparagus mash (see page 34), 1 tablespoon parsnip mash (see page 41) and 1 tablespoon pea mash (see page 40); top with 1 tablespoon finely grated tasty cheese. Give your child as much mash as desired.

**prep + cook time** 5 minutes  **makes** ⅓ cup (4 tablespoons)
**tips**  Reheat single frozen portions of the asparagus, parsnip and pea mash in a microwave oven on MEDIUM (50%) power until just warm, then combine them just before serving. You could also make this mash combination while cooking the individual mashes; freeze in 1-tablespoon batches in ice-cube trays, covered, for up to 1 month.

## mixed vegetable soup

**suitable from 6 months**

Coarsely chop 1 each medium potato, carrot and zucchini. Boil, steam or microwave vegetables until tender; drain. Blend or process vegetables and ½ cup of water until smooth, adding more water if necessary to achieve a soupy consistency. Cool slightly to serve. Give your child as much soup as desired.

**prep + cook time** 15 minutes (+ cooling)
**makes** 2¼ cups (27 tablespoons)
**tips** Store, covered, in the fridge, for up to 2 days. The soup is suitable to freeze, in 1-tablespoon portions in ice-cube trays, covered, for up to 1 month.

## ricotta and spinach purée

**suitable from 6 months**

Boil, steam or microwave 125g (4 ounces) spinach until wilted; drain (if boiling, cool slightly, then wring excess water from the spinach). Cool slightly; blend or process spinach with ½ cup firm ricotta, 1 tablespoon water and a pinch of nutmeg until smooth. Give your child as much purée as desired.

**prep + cook time** 10 minutes (+ cooling)
**makes** ¾ cup (9 tablespoons)
**tips** Store, covered, in the fridge, for up to 2 days. The purée is suitable to freeze, in 1-tablespoon portions in ice-cube trays, covered, for up to 1 month. If you are boiling or steaming the spinach, reserve 1 tablespoon of the cooking water to use later when blending or processing the vegetables for added flavour and nutrients to the purée.

# cauliflower purée

**suitable from 6 months**

Trim 250g (8 ounces) cauliflower; cut into florets. Steam cauliflower about 8 minutes or until tender; drain. Cool slightly; blend or process cauliflower with enough breast milk or cooled boiled water until smooth. Give your child as much cauliflower purée as desired.

**prep + cook time** 15 minutes (+ cooling)
**makes** 1 cup (12 tablespoons)
**tips** Store, covered, in the fridge for up to 2 days. Purée is suitable to freeze, in 1-tablespoon portions in ice-cube trays, covered, for up to 1 month.

# kumara purée

**suitable from 6 months**

Peel and coarsely chop 1 medium kumara (orange sweet potato). Steam kumara for 20 minutes or until tender; drain. Cool slightly; blend or process with approximately 1 tablespoon of breast milk or cooled boiled water until smooth. Give your child as much kumara purée as desired.

**prep + cook time** 25 minutes  (+ cooling)
**makes** 1 cup (12 tablespoons)
**tips** Store, covered, in the fridge for up to 2 days. Purée is suitable to freeze, in 1-tablespoon portions in ice-cube trays, covered, for up to 1 month.

## potato purée

**suitable from 6 months**

Peel and coarsely chop 2 medium potatoes. Steam potato for
20 minutes or until tender; drain. Cool slightly; push potato
through a sieve. Stir in approximately 2 tablespoons of breast
milk or cooled boiled water until smooth. Give your child as
much purée as desired.

**prep + cook time** 25 minutes (+ cooling)
**makes** 1 cup (12 tablespoons)
**tips** Store, covered, in the fridge for up to 2 days. Purée is
suitable to freeze, in 1-tablespoon portions in ice-cube trays,
covered, for up to 1 month.

## pumpkin purée

**suitable from 6 months**

Peel, seed and coarsely chop 400g (12½ ounces) pumpkin.
Steam pumpkin for 12 minutes or until tender; drain. Cool
slightly; push pumpkin through a sieve if needed. Stir in a
little breast milk or cooled boiled water, if needed, until
smooth. Give your child as much purée as desired.

**prep + cook time** 20 minutes  (+ cooling)
**makes** 1 cup (12 tablespoons)
**tips** Store, covered, in the fridge for up to 2 days. Purée is
suitable to freeze, in 1-tablespoon portions in ice-cube trays,
covered, for up to 1 month.

# leek mash

suitable from 6 months

Coarsely chop 1 medium leek. Melt 20g (¾ ounce) butter
in a large frying pan; cook leek, over medium heat, stirring,
for 5 minutes. Add ½ cup salt-reduced vegetable stock; cook,
stirring, for 5 minutes or until leek is tender. Cool slightly;
blend, process or mash leek until the desired consistency is
reached. Give your child as much mash as desired.

**prep + cook time** 15 minutes (+ cooling)
**makes** 1 cup (12 tablespoons)
**tips**  Store, covered, in the fridge for up to 1 day. Leek mash is
suitable to freeze, in 1-tablespoon portions in ice-cube trays,
covered, for up to 1 month.

# pea mash

suitable from 6 months

Steam 250g (8 ounces) frozen peas for 5 minutes or until
tender; drain. Cool slightly; blend, process or mash peas with
approximately 1 tablespoon of breast milk or cooled boiled
water until the desired consistency is reached. Give your
child as much pea mash as desired.

**prep + cook time** 10 minutes (+ cooling)
**makes** 1 cup (12 tablespoons)
**tips**  Store, covered, in the fridge for up to 1 day. Pea mash is
suitable to freeze, in 1-tablespoon portions in ice-cube trays,
covered, for up to 1 month.

# cabbage mash

suitable from 6 months

Finely chop ¼ small cabbage. Place cabbage, ⅓ cup water and
⅓ cup salt-reduced vegetable stock in a medium saucepan;
cook, stirring, until tender. Cool slightly; blend, process or mash
cabbage until the desired consistency is reached. Give your
child as much cabbage mash as desired.

**prep + cook time** 10 minutes (+ cooling)
**makes** 1 cup (12 tablespoons)
**tips** Store, covered, in the fridge for up to 1 day. Cabbage
mash is suitable to freeze, in 1-tablespoon portions in ice-cube
trays, covered, for up to 1 month.

# parsnip mash

suitable from 6 months

Peel and coarsely chop 1 large parsnip. Steam parsnip for
5 minutes or until tender; drain. Cool slightly; blend, process or
mash parsnip with approximately 2 tablespoons of breast milk
or cooled boiled water until the desired consistency is reached.
Give your child as much parsnip mash as desired.

**prep + cook time** 10 minutes (+ cooling)
**makes** 1 cup (12 tablespoons)
**tips** Store, covered, in the fridge for up to 1 day. Parsnip mash
is suitable to freeze, in 1-tablespoon portions in ice-cube trays,
covered, for up to 1 month.

## avocado and cucumber purée

suitable from 6 months

Blend or process 1 coarsely chopped large ripe avocado and 1 peeled, seeded and coarsely chopped lebanese cucumber until smooth. Give your child as much purée as desired.

**prep time** 5 minutes  **makes** 1 cup (12 tablespoons)
**tips**  Store, covered, in the fridge for up to 1 day. Purée is suitable to freeze in 1-tablespoon batches in ice-cube trays, covered, for up to 1 month.

## potato, kumara and parsnip purée

suitable from 6 months

Peel and coarsely chop 1 each small potato, parsnip and kumara (orange sweet potato). Steam the vegetables for 20 minutes or until tender; drain. Cool slightly; push vegetables through a sieve into a small bowl; stir in 1 tablespoon of cooled boiled water. Give your child as much purée as desired.

**prep + cook time** 30 minutes (+ cooling)
**makes** 1 cup (12 tablespoons)
**tips**  Store, covered, in the fridge for up to 1 day. Purée is suitable to freeze in 1-tablespoon batches in ice-cube trays, covered, for up to 1 month.

# ratatouille purée

suitable from 6 months

Heat 2 teaspoons olive oil in a medium saucepan; cook
1 large coarsely chopped zucchini and 1 coarsely chopped
baby eggplant, over medium heat, stirring, for 5 minutes.
Add ½ cup bottled no-added salt tomato pasta sauce and
2 tablespoons water; bring to the boil. Reduce heat; simmer,
covered, for 15 minutes or until vegetables soften. Cool
slightly; blend or process tomato mixture with 2 fresh basil
leaves until smooth. Push through a sieve. Give your child as
much purée as desired.

**prep + cook time** 25 minutes (+ cooling)
**makes** 1 cup (12 tablespoons)
**tips**  Store, covered, in the fridge for up to 1 day. Purée is
suitable to freeze in 1-tablespoon batches in ice-cube trays,
covered, for up to 1 month.

# cauliflower, broccoli and cheese purée

suitable from 6 months

Coarsely chop 100g (3 ounces) cauliflower and 150g (4½ ounces)
broccoli. Steam vegetables until tender; drain. Cool slightly;
blend or process vegetables, ¼ cup coarsely grated cheese
and 2 tablespoons water until smooth. Push through a sieve.
Give your child as much purée as desired.

**prep + cook time** 20 minutes (+ cooling)
**makes** ¾ cup (9 tablespoons)
**tips**  Store, covered, in the fridge for up to 1 day. Purée is
suitable to freeze in 1-tablespoon batches in ice-cube trays,
covered, for up to 1 month.

# patty pan squash purée

## suitable from 6 months

Trim ends and coarsely chop 300g (9½ ounces) patty-pan squash. Steam squash for 12 minutes or until tender; drain. Cool slightly; blend or process squash with a little breast milk or cooled boiled water, if needed, until smooth. Give your child as much purée as desired.

**prep + cook time** 20 minutes (+ cooling)
**makes** 1 cup (12 tablespoons)
**tips** Store, covered, in the fridge for up to 1 day. Purée is suitable to freeze, in 1-tablespoon portions in ice-cube trays, covered, for up to 1 month.

# kumara and squash purée

## suitable from 6 months

Combine 2 tablespoons kumara purée (orange sweet potato) (see page 38) with 1 tablespoon patty-pan squash purée (see page 44). Give your child as much purée as desired.

**prep time** 5 minutes  **makes** ¼ cup (3 tablespoons)
**tips** Reheat frozen portions of vegetable purées in a microwave oven on MEDIUM (50%) power until just warmed. You could make the combination while cooking the purées; freeze in 1-tablespoon batches in ice-cube trays, covered, for up to 1 month.

# sweet corn and pumpkin purée

suitable from 6 months

Combine 2 tablespoons canned creamed corn with
2 tablespoons pumpkin purée (see page 39). Give
your child as much purée as desired.

**prep time** 5 minutes  **makes** ⅓ cup (4 tablespoons)

**tips**  Reheat frozen portions in a microwave oven on
MEDIUM (50%) power until just warmed. You could make
the combination while cooking the purées; freeze, in
1-tablespoon portions in ice-cube trays, covered, for up to
1 month. Freeze remaining creamed corn in 1-tablespoon
batches in ice-cube trays, covered, for up to 1 month.

# potato and pumpkin purée

suitable from 6 months

Combine 2 tablespoons potato purée (see page 39) with
1 tablespoon pumpkin purée (see page 39). Give your child
as much purée as desired.

**prep time** 5 minutes  **makes** ¼ cup (3 tablespoons)

**tips**  Reheat frozen portions in a microwave oven on
MEDIUM (50%) power until just warmed. You could make
the combination while cooking the purées; freeze, in
1-tablespoon portions in ice-cube trays, covered, for
up to 1 month.

# zucchini, pea and corn purée

suitable from 6 months

Coarsely chop 2 small zucchini. Cover zucchini with ¼ cup water in a medium saucepan; add 1 cup each of frozen baby peas and fresh or frozen corn kernels. Cook over medium high heat for 5 minutes or until tender; drain. Reserve 1 tablespoon of the cooking water. Cool slightly; blend or process vegetables and the reserved cooking water until smooth. Give your child as much purée as desired.

**prep + cook time** 15 minutes (+ cooling)
**makes** 1½ cups (18 tablespoons)
**tips** Store, covered, in the fridge for up to 2 days. Purée is suitable to freeze, in 1-tablespoon portions in ice-cube trays, covered, for up to 1 month.

# carrot and spinach purée

suitable from 6 months

Combine 2 tablespoons carrot purée (see page 33) with 1 tablespoon spinach purée (see page 34). Give your child as much purée as desired.

**prep time** 5 minutes  **makes** ¼ cup (3 tablespoons)
**tips**  Reheat frozen portions in a microwave oven on MEDIUM (50%) power until just warmed. You could make the combination while cooking the purées; freeze, in 1-tablespoon portions in ice-cube trays, covered, for up to 1 month.

# carrot and broccoli purée

suitable from 6 months

Combine 2 tablespoons puréed carrot (see page 33) with 1 tablespoon puréed broccoli (see page 33). Give your child as much purée as desired.

**prep time** 5 minutes  **makes** ¼ cup (3 tablespoons)
**tips**  Reheat frozen portions in a microwave oven on MEDIUM (50%) power until just warmed. You could make the combination while cooking the purées; freeze, in 1-tablespoon portions in ice-cube trays, covered, for up to 1 month.

# parsnip, carrot and apple purée

suitable from 6 months

Coarsely chop 1 each medium parsnip, carrot and unpeeled cored apple. Boil parsnip, carrot and apple in a small saucepan for 25 minutes or until tender; drain. Reserve 2 tablespoons of the cooking water. Cool slightly; blend or process cooked mixture with the reserved cooking water until smooth. Push through a sieve. Give your child as much purée as desired.

**prep + cook time** 20 minutes (+ cooling)
**makes** ¾ cup (9 tablespoons)
**tips**  Store, covered, in the fridge, for up to 2 days. Purée is suitable to freeze in 1-tablespoon portions in ice-cube trays, covered, for up to 1 month.

# apple, broccoli and avocado purée

suitable from 6 months

Peel, core and finely chop 1 large green apple. Cut 150g (4½ ounce) broccoli into florets. Boil, steam or microwave apple and broccoli for 15 minutes or until tender; drain. Cool. Meanwhile, blend or process 1 small coarsely chopped avocado until smooth; transfer to a small bowl. Blend or process apple and broccoli mixture with 1 tablespoon of cooled boiled water until smooth, stir into avocado. Give your child as much purée as desired.

**prep + cook**  20 minutes (+ cooling)
**makes**  1 cup (12 tablespoons)
**tips**  Store, covered, in the fridge for up to 1 day. Purée is suitable to freeze, in 1-tablespoon portions in ice-cube trays, covered, for 1 month. If you are boiling or steaming the apple and broccoli, reserve 1 tablespoon of the cooking water to use when blending or processing the ingredients for added flavour and nutrients.

tips  Store, covered, in the fridge for up to 2 days. Purée is suitable to freeze, in 1-tablespoon portions in ice-cube trays, covered, for up to 1 month. If you are boiling or steaming the pumpkin, reserve 1 tablespoon of the cooking water to use later when blending or processing the vegetables for added flavour and nutrients.

# cauliflower, pumpkin and cheddar purée

**suitable from 6 months**

Cut 125g (4 ounces) cauliflower into florets. Coarsely chop 200g (6½ ounces) peeled pumpkin. Boil, steam or microwave vegetables until tender; drain. Cool slightly; blend or process vegetables and 2 tablespoons coarsely grated cheese until smooth. Add 1 tablespoon of cooled boiled water, if necessary, to thin the purée. Cool slightly. Give your child as much purée as desired.

**prep + cook time** 20 minutes (+ cooling)
**makes** 1 cup (12 tablespoons)

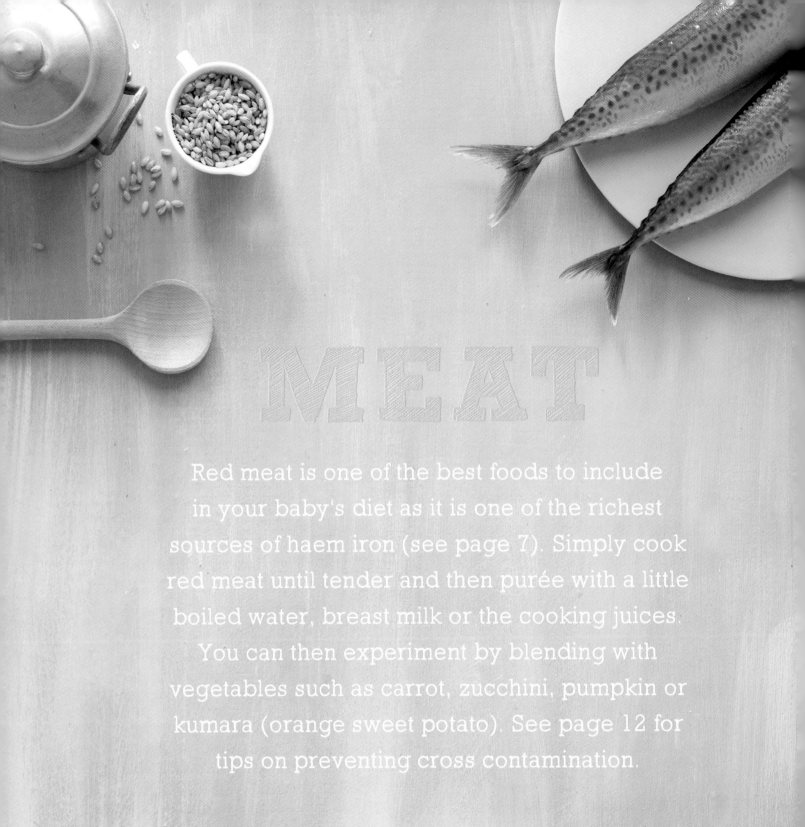

# MEAT

Red meat is one of the best foods to include in your baby's diet as it is one of the richest sources of haem iron (see page 7). Simply cook red meat until tender and then purée with a little boiled water, breast milk or the cooking juices. You can then experiment by blending with vegetables such as carrot, zucchini, pumpkin or kumara (orange sweet potato). See page 12 for tips on preventing cross contamination.

# chicken, barley and vegetable soup

suitable from 8 months

Remove fat from 2 chicken thighs. Place chicken and 1 litre (4 cups) salt-reduced chicken stock in a medium saucepan, bring to the boil; reduce heat, simmer, uncovered, for 30 minutes. Strain over a large bowl; reserve chicken and cooking liquid. Remove meat from chicken thighs, discard bones; set chicken aside. Coarsely chop 1 each small onion and potato, 1 medium carrot and 1 trimmed celery stalk. Return cooking liquid, vegetables and 2 tablespoons pearl barley to the pan; simmer, uncovered, for 30 minutes or until the barley is tender. Return chicken to pan. Cool slightly; blend or process, in batches, until just smooth. Give your child as much soup as desired. Serve with toast, if you like.

**prep + cook time** 1 hour (+ cooling)
**makes** 4 cups (48 tablespoons)

tips Store soup, covered, in the fridge for up to 2 days. Soup is suitable to freeze, in 1-tablespoon portions in ice-cube trays, covered, for up to 1 month.

lamb shank soup

**suitable from 8 months**

Place 1 trimmed lamb shank, 1 each coarsely chopped medium potato and carrot, 1 trimmed, coarsely chopped celery stalk, 1 tablespoon of pearl barley and 1 litre (4 cups) water in a medium saucepan; bring to the boil. Reduce heat to medium. Simmer, covered, for 1 hour or until meat is tender. Cool. When cool enough to handle, remove lamb shank from pan; remove meat from shank; discard bone. Cool slightly; blend or process meat with vegetables, barley and cooking water, in batches, until soup is almost smooth. Give your child as much soup as desired. Serve with bread, if you like.

**prep + cook time** 1¼ hours (+ cooling)
**makes** 4 cups (48 tablespoons)
**tips** Store, covered, in the fridge for up to 2 days. Soup is suitable to freeze, in 1-tablespoon portions in ice-cube trays, covered, for up to 1 month.

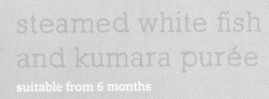

## steamed white fish and kumara purée

**suitable from 6 months**

Place 150g (4½ ounces) skinless firm white fish fillet and 1 small diced kumara (orange sweet potato) in a steamer over a saucepan of simmering water. Cook, covered, for 8 minutes or until fish is cooked through. Transfer fish to a plate. Steam kumara a further 4 minutes or until tender. Cool slightly; blend or process fish and kumara with ⅓ cup of cooled boiled water until smooth. Give your child as much purée as desired.

**prep + cook time** 15 minutes (+ cooling)
**makes** 1¼ cups (15 tablespoons)
**tips** Store, covered, in the fridge for up to 1 day. Purée is suitable to freeze, in 1-tablespoon portions in ice-cube trays, covered, for up to 1 month.

## tuna and broccoli purée

**suitable from 8 months**

Boil, steam or microwave 400g (12½ ounces) broccoli florets until tender; drain. Cool slightly; blend or process broccoli with 180g (5½ ounces) drained canned tuna in spring water and about ¾ cup of water until smooth. Give your child as much purée as desired.

**prep + cook time** 15 minutes (+ cooling)

**makes** 2 cups (24 tablespoons)

**tips** Store, covered, in the fridge for up to 2 days. Purée is suitable to freeze, in 1-tablespoon portions in ice-cube trays, covered, for up to 1 month. If you are boiling the broccoli, reserve 1 cup of the cooking water to use later when blending or processing the ingredients for added flavour and nutrients.

## chicken, zucchini and parsnip purée

**suitable from 6 months**

Place 1 coarsely chopped single chicken breast fillet, 2 small coarsely chopped zucchini, 1 coarsely chopped parsnip and 1¼ cups of water in a small saucepan; bring to the boil. Reduce heat, simmer, uncovered, for 20 minutes until vegetables soften and chicken is cooked through. Cool slightly; blend or process mixture until smooth. Give your child as much purée as desired.

**prep + cook time** 30 minutes (+ cooling)

**makes** 2 cups (24 tablespoons)

**tips** Store, covered, in the fridge for up to 2 days. Purée is suitable to freeze, in 1-tablespoon portions in ice-cube trays, covered, for up to 1 month.

# turkey and pea purée

suitable from 8 months

Combine 100g (3 ounces) diced turkey breast fillet steaks, ¼ small diced red onion and 2 cups of water in a small saucepan; bring to the boil. Reduce heat, simmer, uncovered, for 5 minutes or until turkey is cooked through. Remove turkey with a slotted spoon. Skim foam from surface of the cooking water with a slotted spoon. Reserve ¼ cup of the cooking water. Add 1 cup frozen peas to remaining turkey cooking water; boil until tender. Drain. Blend turkey and peas with reserved cooking water until smooth. Cool slightly to serve. Give your child as much purée as desired.

**prep + cook time** 15 minutes (+ cooling)
**makes** ⅔ cup (8 tablespoons)
**tips** Store, covered, in the fridge for up to 2 days. Purée is suitable to freeze, in 1-tablespoon portions in ice-cube trays, covered, for up to 1 month. Turkey is a fabulous lean source of protein that also contains iron, zinc, B6, niacin and the amino acid tryptophan. Freeze any leftover uncooked turkey breast in 100g portions to use for future purées.

# roast pumpkin and poached chicken purée

suitable from 8 months

Preheat oven to 200°C/400°F. Line an oven tray with baking paper. Place 400g (12½ ounces) diced pumpkin on tray, roast for 20 minutes or until tender; cool. Meanwhile, combine 200g (6½ ounces) diced chicken breast fillet and 2½ cups of water in a small saucepan; bring to the boil. Reduce heat, simmer, uncovered, for 5 minutes or until chicken is cooked through. Skim foam from surface with a slotted spoon. Reserve 1 cup of the poaching liquid. Cool slightly; blend or process pumpkin, chicken and ½ cup of reserved liquid until smooth, adding more only if necessary. Give your child as much purée as desired.

**prep + cook time** 25 minutes (+ cooling)
**makes** 1 cup (12 tablespoons)
**tips** Store, covered, in the fridge for up to 2 days. Purée is suitable to freeze, in 1-tablespoon portions in ice-cube trays, covered, for up to 1 month.

# beef, carrot and kumara purée

suitable from 6 months

Place 150g (4½ ounces) diced beef rump steak, ½ coarsely chopped small kumara (orange sweet potato), 1 coarsely chopped large carrot and 1½ cups of water in a small saucepan; bring to the boil. Reduce heat, simmer, uncovered, for about 20 minutes or until vegetables soften and beef is cooked through. Cool slightly; blend or process mixture until smooth. Give your child as much purée as desired.

**prep + cook time** 30 minutes (+ cooling)
**makes** 2 cups (24 tablespoons)

tips Store, covered, in the fridge for up to 2 days. Purée is suitable to freeze, in 1-tablespoon portions in ice-cube trays, covered, for up to 1 month.

# fish, potato and spinach purée

**suitable from 6 months**

Place 1 coarsely chopped large potato and 1½ cups of water in a small saucepan; bring to the boil. Reduce heat, simmer, uncovered, for 10 minutes or until potato is tender; strain potato over a small bowl. Return liquid to the same pan with 100g (3 ounces) firm white fish fillets and 30g (1 ounce) baby spinach leaves; boil, uncovered, for 5 minutes or until fish is cooked through. Drain; cool. Push potato through a sieve into a small bowl. Blend or process fish and spinach until smooth; stir fish mixture and ¼ cup of extra water into potato. Cool slightly before serving. Give your child as much purée as desired.

**prep + cook time** 30 minutes (+ cooling)
**makes** 2 cups (24 tablespoons)
**tips** Store, covered, in the fridge for up to 1 day. Purée is suitable to freeze, in 1-tablespoon portions in ice-cube trays, covered, for up to 1 month. Don't blend or process the potato as it will become gluey.

# chicken, corn and risoni purée

suitable from 6 months

Combine 100g (3 ounces) coarsely chopped chicken breast fillet, 1¼ cups of water, 1 cup fresh or frozen corn kernels and 1 tablespoon risoni pasta in a small saucepan; bring to the boil. Reduce heat; simmer, uncovered, about 10 minutes or until pasta is tender and chicken is cooked through. Cool slightly; blend or process mixture until smooth. Push through a sieve. Give your child as much purée as desired.

**prep + cook time** 25 minutes (+ cooling)
**makes** 1 cup (12 tablespoons)
**tips** Store, covered, in the fridge for up to 2 days. Purée is suitable to freeze, in 1-tablespoon portions in ice-cube trays, covered, for up to 1 month. If using fresh corn kernels in the purée, you will need about 1 trimmed corn cob (250g) for this recipe.

# chicken livers with pumpkin

suitable from 6 months

Stand 200g (6½ ounces) chicken livers in ½ cup of milk in a small bowl for 30 minutes; drain, discard milk. Separate livers into halves by cutting lobes apart. Meanwhile, boil, steam or microwave 500g (1 pound) coarsely chopped pumpkin until just tender; drain. Heat 1 tablespoon olive oil in a medium frying pan; cook livers, over high heat, for 5 minutes or until cooked through. Drain on absorbent paper towel. Cool slightly; blend or process pumpkin and livers until smooth. Give your child as much purée as desired.

**prep + cook time** 15 minutes (+ standing & cooling)
**makes** 2 cups (24 tablespoons)
**tips** Store, covered, in the fridge for up to 1 day. Purée is suitable to freeze, in 1-tablespoon portions in ice-cube trays, covered, for up to 1 month. Chicken livers are a nutritious source of zinc, iron, vitamin B12, folic acid and vitamin A.

# fish chowder purée

suitable from 6 months

Heat 1 teaspoon olive oil in a small saucepan; cook 1 tablespoon finely chopped rindless bacon and ¼ coarsely chopped celery stalk over medium heat, stirring, for 3 minutes or until celery softens. Add ½ cup breast milk or formula and 1 finely chopped baby new potato; bring to the boil. Simmer, uncovered, stirring occasionally, for 8 minutes or until potato is tender. Add 50g (1½ ounces) coarsely chopped firm white fish fillet; simmer, uncovered, for 2 minutes or until cooked through. Cool slightly; blend or process fish mixture and 3 coarsely chopped fresh chives until smooth. Give your child as much purée as desired.

**prep + cook time** 25 minutes (+ cooling)
**makes** ½ cup (6 tablespoons)
**tips** Store, covered, in the fridge for up to 1 day. This recipe is not suitable to freeze.

# veal mince and bean purée

suitable from 6 months

Heat 1 teaspoon olive oil in a small frying pan; cook 120g (4 ounces) minced (ground) veal, stirring, over medium heat, for 5 minutes or until cooked through. Add ½ cup no-added salt tomato pasta sauce; bring to the boil. Reduce heat; simmer, uncovered, for 3 minutes or until thickened. Cool slightly; blend or process veal mixture with ¼ cup rinsed, drained, canned butter beans, 3 fresh flat-leaf parsley sprigs and 1 tablespoon of water until smooth. Push through a sieve. Give your child as much purée as desired.

**prep + cook time** 15 minutes (+ cooling)
**makes** 1 cup (12 tablespoons)
**tips** Store, covered, in the fridge for up to 2 days. Purée is suitable to freeze, in 1-tablespoon portions in ice-cube trays, covered, for up to 1 month.

# GRAINS

Grains can be offered from 6 months. Because babies now require more iron for growth than breast milk can supply, add legumes (beans, lentils and chickpeas) to the menu as these are a great source of plant iron (see page 7). Quinoa is gluten-free and is also a good source of protein and iron, and contains all the essential amino acids necessary for good health. If not blended until completely smooth, grains offer added texture to food; learning to eat different textures also helps with speech development. For tips on preventing cross contamination when preparing food see page 12.

Store, covered, in the fridge for up to 1 day. Purée is suitable to freeze, in 1-tablespoon portions in ice-cube trays, covered, for up to 1 month. If the purée thickens on standing, thin it with a little water. Quinoa, a seed from a South American plant, is packed with protein and is one of the rare foods that contain all eight amino acids. Delicious blueberries are also high in nutrients.

# blueberry, banana and quinoa purée
suitable from 8 months

Place ⅓ cup quinoa in a fine sieve; rinse thoroughly under cold running water. Drain well. Combine quinoa and ⅔ cup water in a small saucepan; bring to the boil. Reduce heat; simmer, covered, for 12 minutes or until liquid is absorbed and quinoa is tender. Cool slightly; blend or process quinoa with 125g (4 ounces) fresh blueberries, 1 coarsely chopped medium banana and 1 tablespoon extra water until smooth. Push through a sieve. Give your child as much purée as desired.

**prep + cook time** 15 minutes (+ cooling)
**makes** 1½ cups (18 tablespoons)

# quinoa and pumpkin mash

**suitable from 6 months**

Place ⅓ cup white quinoa in a fine sieve; rinse thoroughly under cold running water. Drain well. Combine quinoa and ⅔ cup of water in a small saucepan; bring to the boil. Reduce heat; simmer, covered, for 12 minutes or until liquid is absorbed and quinoa is tender, cool. Boil, steam or microwave 200g (6½ ounces) pumpkin until tender; cool. Combine quinoa, pumpkin and 1 tablespoon of cooled boiled water in a medium bowl; mash to the desired consistency. Give your child as much mash as desired.

**prep + cook time** 20 minutes **makes** 1¾ cups

tips You can use kumara (orange sweet potato) instead of the pumpkin, if you like. Store mash, covered, in the fridge for up to 2 days. Mash is suitable to freeze, in 1-tablespoon portions in ice-cube trays, covered, for up to 1 month. If you are boiling or steaming the pumpkin, reserve 1 tablespoon of the cooking water to use when mashing for added flavour and nutrients.

**suitable from 8 months**

Boil, steam or microwave 2 small diced carrots and 1 cup fresh
or frozen corn kernels, separately, until tender; drain. Blend or
process the vegetables with 400g (12½ ounces) rinsed, drained
canned cannellini beans, 110g (3½ ounces) drained canned
salmon in spring water and ¼ cup of water until smooth. Push
through a sieve. Give your child as much purée as desired.

**prep + cook time** 15 minutes
**makes** 1¾ cups (21 tablespoons)

**tips** Store, covered, in the fridge for up to 2 days. Purée is suitable to
freeze, in 1-tablespoon portions in ice-cube trays, covered, for up to
1 month. If you are boiling or steaming the carrot and corn, reserve
¼ cup of the cooking water to use later when blending and processing
for added flavour and nutrients.

## quick creamed rice

**suitable from 6 months**

Combine ½ cup breast milk or formula and ¼ teaspoon vanilla extract in a small saucepan; bring to the boil, stir in ¼ cup cooked calrose rice. Cook, stirring, for 5 minutes or until thickened. Cool slightly; serve topped with a little ground cinnamon or fruit, if you like. Give your child as much creamed rice as desired.

**prep + cook time** 10 minutes (+ cooling)

**makes** ¾ cup (9 tablespoons)

**tips** Store, covered, in the fridge for up to 2 days. Purée is suitable to freeze, in 1-tablespoon portions in ice-cube trays, covered, for up to 1 month.

## dhal purée

**suitable from 8 months**

Combine ¾ cup of water, 1 each small coarsely chopped carrot and zucchini, 200g (6½ ounces) coarsely chopped pumpkin and 2 tablespoons red lentils in a small saucepan; bring to the boil. Reduce heat; simmer, uncovered, for 15 minutes or until vegetables and lentils are tender. Cool slightly; blend or process mixture until smooth. Push through a sieve. Give your child as much purée as desired.

**prep + cook time** 25 minutes (+ cooling)

**makes** 1 cup (12 tablespoons)

**tips** Store, covered, in the fridge for up to 2 days. Purée is suitable to freeze, in 1-tablespoon portions in ice-cube trays, covered, for up to 1 month.

## oat porridge

**suitable from 6 months**

Combine ⅓ cup rolled oats and ¾ cup breast milk or formula
in a small saucepan; bring to the boil. Reduce heat; simmer,
uncovered, for about 8 minutes or until the liquid is almost
absorbed. Cool slightly. Add a little breast milk, formula or
cooled boiled water to the porridge just before serving if
it is too thick. Give your child as much porridge as desired.

**prep + cook time** 15 minutes (+ cooling)
**makes** ½ cup (6 tablespoons)
**tips** Store, covered, in the fridge for up to 2 days.
Porridge is not suitable to freeze.

## breakfast biscuit

**suitable from 6 months**

Crush 1 whole-wheat malted breakfast biscuit (such as
Weet-bix, Shredded Wheat, etc.) with approximately
2 tablespoons of breast milk, formula or cooled boiled
water until of desired consistency.

**prep time** 5 minutes  **makes** 2 tablespoons
**tip**  Breakfast biscuit is not suitable to freeze.

# red lentil and vegetable mash

suitable from 8 months

Cook ¼ cup red lentils in a small saucepan of boiling water for 6 minutes or until tender; drain. Meanwhile, boil 1 diced medium potato and ½ finely chopped small carrot in a small saucepan for 7 minutes. Add ¼ cup frozen peas; cook for a further 3 minutes or until all vegetables are tender. Reserve ¼ cup of the cooking water, drain. Add water to vegetables and mash until desired consistency is reached. Add lentils to vegetable mixture; stir to combine. Cool slightly. Give your child as much mash as desired.

**prep + cook time** 25 minutes (+ cooling)
**makes** 1 cup (12 tablespoons)

tips  Store, covered, in the fridge for up to 2 days. Purée is suitable to freeze, in 1-tablespoon portions in ice-cube trays, covered, for up to 1 month.

# creamy cheese polenta

Suitable from 8 months

Combine 1 cup of water and 1½ cups milk or formula in a small saucepan; bring to the boil. Gradually add ⅓ cup polenta to liquid, stirring constantly. Reduce heat; simmer, stirring, for 10 minutes or until polenta thickens. Stir in ¼ cup coarsely grated cheddar cheese, cover; cool for 10 minutes, stirring occasionally. Give your child as much polenta as desired.

**prep + cook time** 20 minutes (+ standing)
**makes** 1 cup (12 tablespoons)
**tip** Polenta is not suitable to freeze.

# 9·12 months

Think of this as the finger food stage. Your baby will start to take an interest in feeding her or himself. Allowing them to do so is an important part of their development, messy as it may be. Provide soft, easy to 'gum-chew' foods such as steamed carrot sticks, penne pasta, toast soldiers, cheese sticks, homemade fish fingers, avocado chunks or hard boiled egg cut into quarters. You can also give portions of family meals such as casseroles, penne pasta with bolognese, pilafs and so on – just be sure to cook without added salt as your baby's kidneys cannot yet handle a high salt load.

# BREAKFAST

An important way to start the day: babies not only need energy for their daily activities (just like adults), but also for growth and development. Remember, babies and toddlers have small stomachs, so offer small, regular meals and snacks throughout the day.

## pikelets

1 cup (150g) self-raising flour

2 tablespoons caster (super fine) sugar

1 egg, beaten lightly

¾ cup (180ml) milk, approximately

1 Combine flour and sugar in a medium bowl; gradually whisk in egg and enough milk to make a thick, smooth batter.
2 Heat a greased heavy-based frying pan over medium heat; cook tablespoons of mixture until bubbles begin to appear on the surface of the pikelet. Turn; brown the other side.
3 Serve pikelets with yoghurt and a little stewed or puréed fruit, if you like.

**prep + cook time** 20 minutes **makes** about 22
**tip** These pikelets can be stored in an airtight container for up to 2 days, or freeze for up to 1 month.

This is a great recipe to make as a delicious breakfast for the whole family. Adults can add slices of grilled bacon and tomatoes, and wedges of avocado. Add a dollop of vanilla yoghurt and a drizzle of pure maple syrup for older children.

poached egg

scrambled egg

# poached egg

1 egg

2 teaspoons white vinegar

1 Break egg into a small cup.
2 Bring a small shallow pan of water to a gentle simmer; add vinegar to pan. Use a wooden spoon to make a whirlpool in the water; add the egg. Turn off heat, place lid on pan; stand for 4 minutes or until egg white is just set.
3 Remove with a slotted spoon or egg slide; cool slightly then serve.

**prep + cook time** 8 minutes **serves** 1
**tips** Serve with toast fingers, if you like.

# scrambled egg

1 egg

2 tablespoons milk

5g (¼ ounce) butter

1 Whisk egg and milk in a small bowl.
2 Melt butter in a small frying pan over medium heat. Reduce heat to low; cook egg mixture, stirring, over low heat, until egg sets.

**prep + cook time** 5 minutes **serves** 1
**tips** Serve with toast fingers, if you like.

Eggs contain 11 essential vitamins and minerals and are choc-full of protein. While egg allergy is one of the most common allergies in children, researchers from the University of Melbourne have found that introducing eggs early is thought to provide protection.

# bircher muesli

**Start this recipe the day before.**

⅓ cup (80g) rolled oats

¾ cup (180ml) breast milk or formula

¼ (40g) ripe peach, peeled, seed removed

2 tablespoons milk, extra

**1** Combine oats and milk in a small container, cover; refrigerate overnight.
**2** The next day, mash the peach with a fork. Stir extra milk into the bircher muesli; serve topped with peach. Give your child as much muesli as desired.

**prep time** 5 minutes (+ standing)

**makes** ½ cup (6 tablespoons)

**tip** If you like, add a little grated apple instead of the peach. In winter for a hot porridge, simmer the oats and milk, stirring frequently, over medium heat for 8 minutes or until thickened; stir through the extra milk.

# mango, banana and ricotta

1 small mango (300g), peeled, seeded, coarsely chopped

1 medium banana (200g), peeled, coarsely chopped

¾ cup (180g) firm ricotta

1 Blend or process fruit until smooth.

2 Place fruit in a small bowl, add ricotta; mash with a fork to combine. Give your child as much mash as desired.

**prep time** 10 minutes  **makes** 1¾ cups (21 tablespoons)

**tips**  Store, covered, in the fridge for up to 2 days. Recipe is not suitable to freeze.

9-12 months  77

# muesli

1 whole-wheat malted breakfast biscuit, crushed

¼ cup (10g) bran flakes

¼ cup (10g) rice bubbles

½ cup (75g) finely chopped dried fruit of your choice

2 teaspoons desiccated coconut

**1** Combine all ingredients in medium bowl. Serve with breast milk, formula or yoghurt and chopped fresh fruit, if desired. Give your child as much muesli as desired.

**prep time** 5 minutes  **makes** 1½ cups (18 tablespoons)
**tips** We used dried apples, apricots and sultanas in this version but try experimenting with raisins, dried peaches or dates. Use a breakfast biscuit such as Weet-bix or Shredded Wheat. Muesli can be stored in an airtight container, in the fridge, for up to 3 months.

# LUNCH

Babies need their energy levels topped up in the afternoon: what, with learning to crawl and exploring the saucepan cupboard, life can get pretty busy.

## kumara, coconut milk and rice

¼ cup (50g) basmati rice

1 cup (250ml) water

1 small kumara (orange sweet potato) (250g), peeled, diced

⅓ cup (80ml) coconut milk

1 Place rice in a sieve, rinse well under cold water until water runs clear; drain.
2 Combine rice and the water in a small saucepan; bring to the boil. Reduce heat; cook, covered, for 12 minutes or until liquid is absorbed and rice is tender.
3 Boil, steam or microwave kumara for 10 minutes or until tender.
4 Mash kumara with coconut milk until almost smooth. Stir in rice; mash lightly. Give your child as much rice as desired.

**prep + cook time** 30 minutes  **makes** 1½ cups (18 tablespoons)

Store, covered, in the fridge for up to 2 days. Suitable to freeze in 1-tablespoon batches in ice-cube trays, covered, for up to 1 month. It's better to slightly overcook the rice so it has a soft, creamy texture.

tofu and vegetable patties

zucchini and corn pasta

# tofu and vegetable patties

1 tablespoon mashed silken tofu

1 tablespoon kumara purée (orange sweet potato) (see page 38)

1 tablespoon carrot purée (see page 33)

1 tablespoon zucchini, pea and corn purée (see page 46)

2 teaspoons rice flour

1 Combine ingredients in a small bowl; shape into two patties.
2 Heat a lightly oiled small non-stick frying pan over medium heat; cook patties, uncovered, for 3 minutes each side or until heated through and browned lightly.

**prep + cook time** 20 minutes  **makes** 2
**tip**  Any leftover mashed vegetables can be used to make the tofu and vegetable patties, just be sure to use a total of ¼ cup (3 tablespoons) of mash along with the 2 teaspoons of rice flour.

# zucchini and corn pasta

20g (¾ ounces) butter

1 small tomato (50g), chopped finely

1 small zucchini (90g), grated coarsely

⅓ cup (60g) risoni pasta

2 tablespoons creamed corn

1 Melt butter in a small saucepan; cook tomato and zucchini, stirring, over medium heat, until vegetables are tender.
2 Meanwhile, cook risoni in a medium saucepan of boiling water until tender; drain.
3 Combine warm risoni and vegetable mixture with corn in a small bowl.

**prep + cook time** 12 minutes  **makes** 2 cups (24 tablespoons)
**tips**  Store, covered, in the fridge for up to 2 days. Recipe is suitable to freeze, in 1-tablespoon portions in ice-cube trays, covered, for up to 1 month. Risoni is a small rice-shape pasta available from most supermarkets and Italian delicatessens.

# baked ricotta with tomato sauce

400g (12½ ounces) ricotta

1 tablespoon finely chopped fresh oregano

1 tablespoon olive oil

1 clove garlic, crushed

425g (13½ ounces) canned diced tomatoes

½ cup (130g) bottled no-added salt tomato pasta sauce

1 teaspoon white (granulated) sugar

1 Preheat oven to 160°C/325°F. Line an oven tray with baking paper.

2 Combine the ricotta and oregano in a small bowl; shape mixture into four patties. Place on the baking tray; drizzle with half the oil. Bake, uncovered, for 20 minutes or until heated through.

3 Meanwhile, heat remaining oil in a small saucepan; cook garlic, stirring, over medium heat, for 1 minute. Add tomatoes, pasta sauce and sugar; bring to the boil. Reduce heat; simmer, uncovered, stirring occasionally, for 15 minutes or until sauce thickens. Serve sauce with baked ricotta.

**prep + cook time** 30 minutes  **makes** 4

**tip**  Leftover baked ricotta can be used in pasta, a frittata or on pizza.

# vegetable and cheese tarts

**1 sheet shortcrust pastry**

½ **small tomato (65g), chopped finely**

½ **small carrot (35g), chopped finely**

½ **small zucchini (45g), chopped finely**

¼ **cup (50g) rinsed, drained canned kidney beans**

**2 tablespoons frozen peas, thawed**

⅔ **cup (80g) finely grated cheddar**

**1** Preheat oven to 200°C/400°F.
**2** Cut pastry into nine 7cm (2¾-inch) rounds; press pastry rounds into nine holes of a greased shallow round-based (1½-tablespoon/30ml) patty pan, prick bases well with a fork.
**3** Bake pastry cases for 15 minutes or until browned lightly; remove from oven. Reduce oven temperature to 180°C/350°F.
**4** Meanwhile, combine tomato, carrot, zucchini, beans and peas in a small bowl; divide mixture among pastry cases, sprinkle cheese over top of each tart. Bake for 10 minutes or until cheese melts.

**prep + cook time** 45 minutes  **makes** 9
**tips**  Store, covered, in the fridge for 1 day.
Unfilled pastry cases can be frozen for up to 1 month.

# chickpeas, carrot and cauliflower mash

**1 large carrot (180g), diced**

**125g (4 ounces) cauliflower, cut into florets**

**400g (12½ ounces) canned chickpeas, rinsed, drained**

**½ cup (125ml) hot water**

**1** Boil, steam or microwave carrot and cauliflower until tender.
**2** Stir chickpeas and vegetables in a small saucepan, over low heat, for 5 minutes or until heated through.
**3** Mash chickpea mixture with the water until the desired consistency is reached.

**prep + cook time** 15 minutes  **makes** 1¾ cups (21 tablespoons)

tips  Store, covered, in the fridge for up to 2 days. Recipe is suitable to freeze, in 1-tablespoon portions in ice-cube trays, covered, for up to 1 month. If you are boiling or steaming the vegetables, reserve ¹/₂ cup of the cooking liquid to add to the mash for added flavour and nutrients.

# corn and bacon fritters

4 rindless bacon slices (260g), chopped finely

2 cups (320g) fresh corn kernels

2 green onions, chopped finely

⅔ cup (100g) plain (all-purpose) flour

½ teaspoon bicarbonate of soda (baking soda)

⅔ cup (160ml) buttermilk

2 eggs

125g (4 ounces) canned creamed corn

½ cup (140g) tomato sauce

1 Cook bacon in a large non-stick frying pan, over medium heat, until crisp. Add corn kernels and onion; cook, stirring, for 2 minutes. Remove from heat.

2 Sift flour and soda into a medium bowl. Make a well in the centre; gradually whisk in combined buttermilk and eggs, whisking until batter is smooth. Stir in bacon mixture and creamed corn.

3 Pour ¼ cup batter into the same heated oiled frying pan. Using a spatula, spread the batter into a round shape. Cook, two at a time, over medium heat, for 2 minutes each side or until fritters are browned lightly and cooked through. Remove fritters from pan; cover to keep warm. Repeat process with remaining batter.

4 Divide fritters among serving plates; serve with tomato sauce.

**prep + cook time** 35 minutes  **serves** 4

**tips**  You need 2 fresh corn cobs for this recipe, or use the same amount of canned corn kernels. Fritters are suitable to freeze, in an airtight container, for up to 1 month.

## mashed white beans and zucchini

400g (12½ ounces) canned cannellini beans, rinsed, drained

1 medium zucchini (120g), coarsely grated

⅓ cup (80ml) water

**1** Combine beans, zucchini and the water in a small saucepan; cook, stirring occasionally, over low heat, for 8 minutes or until heated through.

**2** Mash to desired consistency, add a little extra water if required. Cool before serving.

**prep + cook time** 10 minutes (+ cooling)

**makes** 1 cup (12 tablespoons)

**tips** Store, covered, in the fridge for up to 2 days. Suitable to freeze, in 1-tablespoon portions in ice-cube trays, covered, for up to 1 month. You could also add ¼ cup (20g) finely grated parmesan or cheddar cheese to the mixture when mashing.

## salmon quichettes

1 sheet shortcrust pastry

½ cup (60g) coarsely grated cheddar

105g (3½ ounces) canned red salmon, drained, flaked

¼ cup (60ml) milk

1 egg

**1** Preheat oven to 200°C/400°F.

**2** Cut pastry into nine 7.5cm (3-inch) rounds; press pastry rounds into nine holes of a greased shallow round-based (1½-tablespoon/30ml) patty pan.

**3** Divide combined cheese and salmon among pastry cases. Whisk milk and egg together in a small jug; pour enough egg mixture into each pastry case to cover filling. Bake for about 20 minutes or until filling is set. Cool for 5 minutes before removing quichettes from pan. Cool until warm before serving.

**prep + cook time** 40 minutes (+ cooling) **makes** 9

**tip** Recipe is best made just before serving.

mashed white beans and zucchini

salmon quichettes

# DINNER

Try a wider variety of flavours and coarser textures; move away from simple purées and offer mashes, pasta, minced meats, lentils and grains.

## salmon and tomato pasta

½ cup (30g) small soup pasta

1 cup (270g) crushed canned tomatoes

1 tablespoon canned drained salmon

1 small zucchini (90g), grated finely

**1** Cook pasta in a medium saucepan of boiling water until tender; drain.

**2** Meanwhile, combine tomatoes and salmon in a small saucepan over medium heat; cook, stirring occasionally, for 5 minutes or until heated through, breaking salmon up with a spoon. Stir in zucchini.

**3** Add pasta to tomato mixture and stir to combine. Cool slightly to serve.

**prep + cook time** 20 minutes **makes** 1½ cups (18 tablespoons)
**tips** Pasta is best eaten on the day it is made. Suitable to freeze, in 1-tablespoon portions in ice-cube trays, covered, for up to 1 month. You can use any small shaped pasta, such as macaroni, ditali rigati (tiny short tubes) or stelline (tiny stars). Slightly overcook the pasta so it's softer for your baby to eat.

turkey meatballs with simple tomato sauce

red kidney beans, beef and spinach

# turkey meatballs with simple tomato sauce

2 slices white bread (90g), crusts removed

⅓ cup (80ml) buttermilk

500g (1 pound) turkey or chicken mince

2 tablespoons finely grated parmesan

½ small brown onion (40g), grated coarsely

½ small carrot (35g), grated finely

½ small zucchini (45g), grated finely

700g (1½ pounds) bottle no-added salt tomato passata

¼ cup (60ml) water

1 Place bread in a small bowl, pour over buttermilk; leave to soak for 5 minutes.
2 Combine bread mixture, turkey, parmesan and vegetables in a medium bowl. Roll slightly rounded tablespoons of the mixture into balls. Place on a tray lined with plastic wrap; refrigerate for 30 minutes.
3 Combine passata and the water in a medium saucepan over medium heat; bring to a simmer.
4 Carefully drop meatballs into the sauce, swirling the pan to ensure meatballs are submerged, slowly simmer sauce for 10 minutes or until meatballs are cooked through.

prep + cook time 45 minutes (+ refrigeration) makes 36 balls
tips Store, covered, in the fridge for up to 2 days. Freeze in individual portions. Don't make the meatballs the size of cherry tomatoes or grapes, as that size can represent a choking hazard to babies. Older babies might like to use their fingers to eat these, while for younger ones, the meatballs can be mashed with a fork. You can substitute chicken, beef, veal and pork mince for turkey, if you like.

# red kidney beans, beef and spinach

150g (4½ ounces) beef rump steak, diced

1½ cups (375ml) water

40g (1½ ounces) baby spinach leaves

400g (12½ ounces) canned red kidney beans, rinsed, drained

1 Place beef and the water in a small saucepan; bring to the boil. Boil for 3 minutes or until beef is cooked through. Skim foam from the surface with a slotted spoon. Stir spinach into pan; cook for 1 minute or until wilted. Reserve ½ cup of the cooking water; drain.
2 Blend or process beef and spinach with the kidney beans, adding only enough of the reserved cooking water until you have the desired consistency.

prep + cook time 15 minutes  makes 1 cup (12 tablespoons)
tips Store, covered, in the fridge for up to 2 days. Suitable to freeze, in 1-tablespoon portions in ice-cube trays, covered, for up to 1 month.

# roasted butterflied chicken with mash and corn

*This recipe is great as a family meal. Cooking for the whole family is important as it reduces the time you spend in the kitchen. Encourage your toddler to eat what you are eating.*

1.6kg (3¼ pound) whole chicken

30g (1 ounce) butter, softened

1 teaspoon finely chopped fresh thyme

2 teaspoons finely grated lemon rind

3 trimmed corn cobs (750g), quartered

creamy mash

800g (1½ pounds) potatoes, chopped coarsely

⅔ cup (160ml) warm milk (see tips)

20g (¾ ounce) butter

1 Preheat oven to 220°C/425°F.

2 Using kitchen scissors, cut down both sides of the chicken's backbone; discard backbone. Place chicken, skin-side up, on a board; using the heel of your hand, press down hard on the breastbone to flatten chicken. (Or ask the butcher to butterfly the chicken for you.)

3 Combine butter, thyme and rind in a small bowl. Loosen the skin of the chicken by sliding your fingers between the skin and the meat at the neck joint. Push butter mixture under the skin.

4 Place chicken on a lightly oiled wire rack in a large shallow baking dish; roast, uncovered, for 45 minutes or until chicken is cooked through.

5 Meanwhile, make creamy mash. Boil, steam, or microwave corn until tender; drain.

6 Serve chicken with corn and creamy mash. Cool slightly before serving to your baby.

**creamy mash** Boil, steam or microwave potato until tender; drain. Mash potato in large bowl with milk and butter.

**prep + cook time** 1 hour **serves** 4

tips  Set some of the boiled potato aside and mash with a little breast milk or formula for your baby. For older babies, remove the kernels from one corn cob quarter and chop them with a small piece of chicken meat. Serve with a few tablespoons of creamy mash. For younger babies, blend or process the chicken and corn.

green beans, basil, lamb and couscous

spaghetti bolognese

# spaghetti bolognese

1 large brown onion (200g), chopped finely

500g (1 pound) minced (ground) beef

520g (1 pound) bottled chunky no-added salt tomato pasta sauce

375g (12 ounces) spaghetti

1 Cook onion in a heated oiled large frying pan over high heat, stirring, for 3 minutes or until soft and browned lightly.
2 Add mince; cook, stirring, for 5 minutes or until browned. Stir in pasta sauce; cook over medium heat, uncovered, for 10 minutes or until mixture thickens, stirring occasionally.
3 Meanwhile, cook pasta in a large saucepan of boiling water until tender; drain.
4 Serve spaghetti topped with bolognese sauce. Top with grated parmesan or cheddar, if you like.

**prep + cook time** 30 minutes **serves** 4
**tip** This will feed a family of four. Chop the spaghetti into small pieces for toddlers. Any leftover bolognese can be frozen in individual portions for up to 3 months. Bolognese is the most well-known and best loved of all the pasta sauces, especially by kids.

# green beans, basil, lamb and couscous

100g (3 ounces) diced lamb

1½ cups (375ml) cold water

150g (4½ ounces) green beans, trimmed, chopped coarsely

¼ cup (50g) couscous

¼ cup (60ml) boiling water

10g (½ ounces) butter (optional)

¼ cup loosely packed basil leaves, coarsely chopped

1 Place lamb and the cold water in a small saucepan; bring to the boil. Add beans, boil for 3 minutes or until meat is cooked through and beans are tender. Reserve ½ cup of the cooking water. Drain.
2 Combine couscous, butter (if using) and the boiling water in a small heatproof bowl. Cover; stand for 5 minutes or until liquid is absorbed; fluff with a fork. Cool slightly.
3 Blend or process lamb, reserved cooking water, beans and basil until smooth. Cool slightly; push through a sieve. Stir through couscous.

**prep + cook time** 15 minutes **makes** 1¼ cups (15 tablespoons)
**tips** Store, covered, in the fridge for up to 2 days. Suitable to freeze, in 1-tablespoon portions in ice-cube trays, covered, for up to 1 month. As your baby becomes more accustomed to a wider range of vegetables, you can introduce them to mild herbs, such as basil and parsley, to develop their sense of taste even further.

At 8 months, you can introduce more coarsely-textured food. Children will eat when they're hungry, so don't be discouraged if at first they refuse new foods; add them to more familiar dishes.

Store, covered, in the fridge for up to 2 days. Suitable to freeze, in 1-tablespoon batches in ice-cube trays, covered, for up to 1 month. Introducing a range of flavours into your baby's diet not only make sense nutritionally, but has been shown to increase their acceptance of a wider range of flavours later on in life.

## chicken, rice and buk choy mash

¼ cup (50g) basmati rice

100g (3 ounces) chicken breast fillet, diced

1¾ cups (430ml) water

150g (4½ ounces) buk choy, chopped finely

**1** Rinse rice under cold running water thoroughly, until water runs clear; drain.
**2** Bring chicken and the water to the boil in a small saucepan. Reduce heat to medium; simmer for 2 minutes. Add buk choy, cook a further 2 minutes or until chicken is cooked through.
**3** Using a slotted spoon, transfer the chicken and buk choy to a food processor or blender; set aside.
**4** Add rice to the cooking water; bring to the boil. Boil for 12 minutes or until rice is slightly overcooked. Reserve ¼ cup cooking liquid; drain.
**5** Blend or process chicken and buk choy, with a little of the reserved cooking liquid, until mash is of the desired consistency. Stir in rice; mash lightly.

**prep + cook time** 25 minutes  **makes** 1 cup (12 tablespoons)
**tip** Recipe is not suitable to freeze.

# carrot and lentil soup

1 tablespoon ground cumin

6 large carrots (1kg), chopped coarsely

2 trimmed celery sticks (200g), chopped coarsely

½ cup (100g) brown lentils

**1** Heat an oiled large saucepan. Add cumin, carrot and celery; cook over medium heat, stirring, 2 minutes.

**2** Add 1.5 litres (6 cups) water to pan; bring to the boil. Reduce heat; simmer, uncovered, for 20 minutes or until vegetables are tender. Cool 10 minutes.

**3** Blend or process mixture, in batches, until smooth. Return mixture to pan; add lentils. Simmer, uncovered, for 20 minutes or until lentils are tender.

**prep + cook time** 1 hour  **serves** 6

**tips**  Store, covered, in the fridge for up to 2 days. Freeze soup in ¼-cup batches, covered, for up to 1 month. There's a lot to love about lentils: they're nutty and earthy in flavour, high in dietary fibre, low in kilojoules, and a good source of protein and vitamin B.

**serving suggestion**  A dollop of sour cream and some fresh crusty bread rolls.

# risoni with mixed vegetables

1 small red capsicum (bell pepper) (150g), chopped finely

1 large zucchini (150g), chopped finely

310g (10 ounces) canned corn kernels, rinsed, drained

400g (12½ ounces) canned crushed tomatoes

2 tablespoons risoni pasta

**1** Cook capsicum in a lightly oiled frying pan, over medium heat, stirring, for 3 minutes. Add zucchini and corn; cook, stirring, for 2 minutes. Add tomatoes; cook, stirring occasionally, for 15 minutes or until vegetables soften. Cool slightly; blend or process until smooth.
**2** Meanwhile, cook risoni in a small saucepan of boiling water until tender; drain.
**3** To serve, toss risoni with ¼ cup of the vegetable mixture.

**prep + cook time** 20 minutes
**makes** ⅓ cup risoni and 1½ cups vegetable mixture
**tips** Freeze the vegetable mixture in ¼-cup batches, covered, for up to 1 month. Cook more risoni when reheating vegetables. Risoni is a small rice-shape pasta.

chicken and vegetable soup

fish in cheese sauce

# chicken and vegetable soup

2 teaspoons vegetable oil

2 green onions, sliced thinly

1 clove garlic, crushed

2 cups (500ml) chicken stock

2 cups (500ml) water

350g (11 ounces) chicken mince

1 tablespoon cornflour (cornstarch)

¼ cup (60ml) water, extra

310g (11 ounces) canned creamed corn

1 cup (160g) fresh corn kernels

100g (3 ounces) snow peas, trimmed, sliced thinly

1 egg, beaten lightly

1 Heat oil in a large saucepan; cook onion and garlic, stirring, over medium heat, until onion softens. Add stock and the water; bring to the boil. Add chicken, reduce heat to low; simmer, stirring, for 5 minutes or until chicken is cooked through.
2 Blend cornflour and the extra water in a small jug; add to pan with creamed corn, corn kernels and snow peas. Cook, stirring, until mixture boils and thickens. Blend or process a small portion of the soup at this stage for the toddler; leave the remaining soup unblended for the rest of the family.
3 Just before serving, gradually add egg to the remaining soup (family portion) in a thin stream.

**prep + cook time** 30 minutes  **serves** 4
**tips**  This soup will feed a family of four. Soup, without the egg, can be frozen in individual portions for up to 2 months.

# fish in cheese sauce

10g (½ ounce) butter

2 teaspoons plain (all-purpose) flour

½ cup (125ml) breast milk or formula

2 tablespoons finely grated cheddar

30g (1 ounce) skinless, boneless flathead fillet

1 tablespoon small broccoli florets

1 Melt butter in a small saucepan over medium heat, add flour; cook, stirring, until mixture bubbles and thickens. Gradually add milk; cook, stirring, until sauce boils and thickens slightly. Remove from heat; stir in cheese.
2 Meanwhile, boil, steam or microwave fish and broccoli, separately, until broccoli is tender and fish is cooked through; drain well.
3 Flake fish into small chunks, carefully removing any bones that have been missed; combine fish, broccoli and 1 tablespoon of the cheese sauce in a small bowl. Cool slightly before serving.

**prep + cook time** 20 minutes
**makes** 1 cup cheese sauce (12 tablespoons)
**tips**  Cheese sauce can also be used on mashed vegetables, puréed chicken or pasta. Freeze the remaining cheese sauce in 1-tablespoon batches in ice-cube trays, covered, for up to 1 month. Any firm fresh white fish can be used.

# Snacks

## fruit jelly

Place ¼ cup of fruit juice in a heatproof cup; sprinkle over 3 teaspoons of gelatine. Stand cup in a small pan of simmering water; stir until gelatine is dissolved. Pour an extra 1¾ cups of fruit juice into a medium bowl; stir gelatine mixture into juice. Refrigerate until firm; give your child as much jelly as desired.

**prep + cook time** 10 minutes (+ refrigeration) **makes** 2 cups
**tips** This is a soft-set jelly. You need a total of 2 cups (500ml) fruit juice for this recipe. Use any type of fruit juice you like. We recommend you use 100% fruit juice that doesn't contain added sugar. Recipe is not suitable to freeze.

## stewed fruit compote

Peel, quarter and thickly slice 1 small pear. Combine pear in a medium saucepan with 2 cups water, ⅓ cup dried apricots, ⅓ cup seeded prunes, 1 cinnamon stick and 1 tablespoon brown sugar; simmer, covered, for 20 minutes or until fruit is tender. Cool; discard cinnamon stick. Mash fruit, serve with yoghurt, if you like. Give your child as much compote as desired.

**prep + cook time** 30 minutes (+ cooling)
**makes** about 2 cups (24 tablespoons)
**tip** Store, covered, in the fridge for up to 2 days. Suitable to freeze, in 1-tablespoon portions in ice-cube trays, covered, for up to 1 month.

## fruit muffins

Preheat oven to 200°C/400°F. Grease three 12-hole
(1 tablespoon/20ml) mini muffin pans. Combine 2 cups
(300g) self-raising flour, 1 teaspoon mixed spice, ½ cup (110g)
firmly packed brown sugar and ½ cup (80g) sultanas in a large
bowl. Stir in 1 cup milk, 125g (4 ounces) melted butter and
1 lightly beaten egg; do not over-mix (the batter should be
coarse and slightly lumpy). Divide mixture into pan holes;
bake about 15 minutes. Stand muffins in pans for 5 minutes
before turning, top-side up, onto wire racks to cool.

**prep + cook time** 25 minutes **makes** 36
**tips**  Store in an airtight container for up to 2 days. Freeze
muffins for up to 2 months. Vary the flavour by changing the
dried fruit to chopped dried apricots, raisins, seeded dates
or seeded prunes, or a combination of any of these.

## mango, pineapple and orange ice-blocks

Peel, core and coarsely chop 1 medium pineapple (1.25kg).
Peel, seed and coarsely chop 1 small mango (300g). Blend or
process pineapple and mango until smooth. Using a wooden
spoon, push mixture through a fine sieve or mouli into a large
bowl. Stir in ½ cup orange juice. Pour mixture into 8 x ⅓-cup
(80ml) ice-block moulds. Freeze for 3 hours or until firm.

**prep time** 20 minutes (+ freezing) **makes** 8
**tip** Store frozen ice-blocks for up to 2 months.

# PARTY FOOD

We all know the first birthday party is mainly for parents and friends, rather than the child, but the recipes here will suit younger children. Make sure that you have cocktail franks, fairy bread and party pies on hand for nostalgic adults.

## cheesy pastry twists

2 sheets puff pastry, thawed

1 egg yolk, beaten

1 cup (100g) coarsely grated pizza cheese

½ cup (40g) finely grated parmesan

**1** Preheat oven to 200°C/400°F. Oil two oven trays; line with baking paper.

**2** Brush one pastry sheet with half of the egg yolk; sprinkle with pizza cheese. Top with remaining pastry sheet; brush with remaining egg yolk. Sprinkle with parmesan. Cut pastry stack in half; place one pastry half on top of the other, pressing down firmly to seal.

**3** Cut pastry widthways into 24 strips; twist each, pinching ends to seal. Place twists on trays; bake for 10 minutes or until browned lightly.

**prep + cook time** 30 minutes **makes** 24

**tip** The cheesy pastry twists can be cut and twisted into any shape you like. Freeze uncooked twists for up to 1 month. Cooked twists can be stored in an airtight container for up to 2 days.

You don't need a wide variety of food at a birthday party for a one year old – after all, these are the little people who, at this stage, prefer the wrapping paper and the box to the actual gift inside. Just make sure you have a few different textures. It is essential that it's all finger food, though – no one, not even adults, will stay seated long enough to partake in a sit-down meal.

## watermelon and strawberry ice-blocks

⅓ cup (80ml) water

2 tablespoons white (granulated) sugar

350g (11 ounces) watermelon

80g (2½ ounces) strawberries

2 teaspoons lemon juice

1 Combine water and sugar in a small saucepan; stir over low heat until sugar dissolves. Bring to the boil; boil, uncovered, without stirring, for 2 minutes or until mixture thickens slightly. Transfer syrup to a small bowl; refrigerate until cold.

2 Peel and remove seeds from watermelon; coarsely chop flesh. Hull and coarsely chop strawberries.

3 Blend or process cold syrup with watermelon, strawberries and lemon juice until smooth. Pour mixture into four ⅓-cup (80ml) ice-block moulds. Freeze ice-blocks until firm, stirring occasionally during freezing to stop mixture from separating.

prep + cook time 15 minutes (+ refrigeration & freezing)
makes 4
tips Ice-blocks can be frozen for up to 1 month. For a smaller treat for younger babies, freeze in ice-cube containers with ice-block sticks.

# sticky chicken drummettes

¾ cup (180ml) tomato sauce

⅓ cup (80ml) plum sauce

2 tablespoons worcestershire sauce

1 tablespoon brown sugar

16 chicken drummettes (1kg)

**1** Combine sauces and sugar in a large bowl; add chicken. Cover; refrigerate for 3 hours or overnight.
**2** Preheat oven to 200°C/400°F.
**3** Drain chicken; discard marinade. Place chicken on an oiled wire rack over a large baking dish. Roast for 30 minutes or until cooked through.

**prep + cook time** 40 minutes (+ refrigeration) **makes** 16
**tip** Marinate the chicken up to a day before the party. Roast the chicken up to an hour before serving – don't forget to deal with the guests small sticky fingers. Chicken drummette is the small fleshy part of the chicken wing between the shoulder and the elbow, trimmed to resemble a drumstick.

# chicken and vegetable rolls

500g (1 pound) chicken mince

1 clove garlic, crushed

1 medium brown onion (150g), chopped finely

1 medium carrot (120g), chopped finely

100g (3 ounces) green beans, trimmed, chopped finely

125g (4 ounces) canned creamed corn

1 egg, beaten lightly

⅓ cup (25g) stale breadcrumbs

1 tablespoon tomato sauce

3 sheets ready-rolled puff pastry

1 egg, beaten lightly, extra

**1** Preheat oven to 200°C/400°F. Oil two oven trays.
**2** Use your hand to combine the mince, garlic, onion, carrot, beans, corn, egg, breadcrumbs and sauce in a large bowl.
**3** Cut pastry sheets in half lengthways. Place equal amounts of chicken mixture lengthways down long edge of each pastry piece; roll over to enclose filling in pastry. Cut each roll into six pieces. Place, seam-side down, on trays; brush with extra egg.
**4** Bake rolls for 30 minutes or until browned lightly and cooked through.

**prep + cook time** 45 minutes **makes** 36
**tip** Uncooked rolls can be frozen for up to 2 months. Add an extra 15-20 minutes to the cooking time if cooking from frozen.
**serving suggestion** Serve with tomato or barbecue sauce.

sticky chicken drummettes

chicken and vegetable rolls

toastie men

fruity rockets

# toastie men

14 slices white bread (630g)

14 slices wholemeal bread (630g)

250g (8 ounces) spreadable cream cheese

70g (2½ ounces) shaved ham, chopped finely

1 tablespoon finely chopped fresh chives

95g (3 ounces) canned tuna in spring water, drained

1 tablespoon finely chopped cornichons

1 tablespoon finely chopped fresh flat-leaf parsley

**1** Preheat grill (broiler).
**2** Using a small gingerbread man cutter, cut three 5cm (2-inch) men from each bread slice; place on oven trays. Grill bread, in batches, until browned both sides.
**3** Divide cream cheese into two small bowls; stir ham and chives into one bowl, and stir tuna, cornichons and parsley into remaining bowl.
**4** Spread level teaspoons of ham mixture onto each white toast; spread level teaspoons of tuna mixture onto each wholemeal toast.

**prep + cook time** 45 minutes  **makes** 42 of each
**tips**  You can make toasts one day ahead and store in an airtight container. Make fillings one day ahead and store, covered, in the fridge. Assemble the toastie men several hours before the party.

# fruity rockets

2 small apples (260g)

2 medium kiwifruit (170g), peeled

1 large orange (300g), peeled

1 small banana (130g)

6 small strawberries (90g), hulled

**1** Carefully remove cores from apples, keeping the hole as small and as neat as possible. Cut each apple and kiwifruit crossways into three slices. Cut a 5.5cm (2½ -inch) circle from each apple slice. Cut orange and banana crossways into six slices.
**2** Place orange slices on serving plates; top each with an apple round, a slice of kiwifruit, banana and then strawberry.

**prep time** 15 minutes  **makes** 6
**tips**  The apples and banana will need to be cut as close to serving as possible as they discolour quite fast once cut. If you like, you can sprinkle the cut banana and apple with lemon juice to help prevent the discolouration.

# one duck family all in a row

You need 3.5cm (1½-inch) and 6.5cm (2¾-inch) wide
duck-shaped cutters, a new small artist's paint brush, and
a 20cm x 50cm (8-inch x 20-inch) rectangular cake board.

½ x 470g (15-ounce) packet butter cake mix (see tips)

100g (3-ounce) ready-made white icing

pure icing (confectioners') sugar, for dusting

yellow, orange and blue food colouring

blue writing icing

butter cream

60g (2 ounces) butter, softened

¾ cup (120g) icing (confectioners') sugar

1 tablespoon milk

1 Preheat oven to 180°C/350°F. Line six holes of a 12-hole
(⅓-cup/80ml) standard muffin pan with blue paper cases.
2 Make cake according to directions on packet. Drop 2½ level
tablespoons of mixture into each paper case; bake for about
20 minutes. Stand cakes in pan for 5 minutes before turning,
top-side up, onto a wire rack to cool.
3 Knead ready-made icing on a surface dusted with a little
sifted icing sugar until icing loses its stickiness; tint yellow. Roll
icing on a surface dusted with a little sifted icing sugar into a
3mm (⅛-inch) thickness. Using cutters, cut two large ducks and
five small ducks from the icing. Using the artist's brush one side
of a large duck sparingly, but evenly, with water. Gently press
the other large duck onto the damp surface.
4 Using the brush and orange food colouring, paint an orange
beak on each side of the mother duck's head. Lay mother duck
flat on a baking-paper-lined tray to dry. Paint beaks on ducklings;
dry on tray with mother duck. Using writing icing, dot blue
eyes on all the ducks.
5 Make butter cream. Spread butter cream over tops of cakes.
Position cakes on the cake board to resemble the number 1;
secure to board with a little butter cream. Position mother
duck and ducklings on cakes.

**butter cream** Beat butter in a small bowl with an electric mixer
until as white as possible. Gradually beat in half the sifted icing
sugar, milk then remaining icing sugar. Tint butter cream blue.

**prep + cook time** 2 hours (+ cooling) **serves** 6
**tip** Make the whole cake and use to make a duckling-topped
cake for each small guest – even though they might not be
eating the cakes they'll love the look of them. Make sure the
ducks are completely dry and firm. The drying time will depend
on the weather; if it's wet or humid, it could take overnight.
The ducklings will take less time to dry than the mother duck.

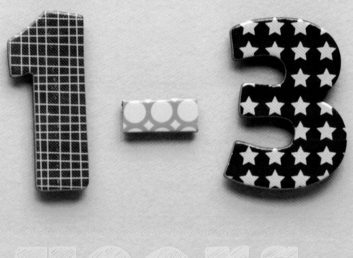

# 1-3 years

Welcome to the toddler years! This can see the emergence of fussy eaters and tantrums over food as toddlers exert some control over their environment. Don't allow bad habits to become ingrained. Keep mealtimes as pleasant as possible. Have the family eat together when possible, as toddlers learn through imitation. They should now be eating most regular family meals, with some adaptations (most of these recipes will feed a family of 4). Regular full-fat cow's milk can now be used as a drink, but be careful not to allow your toddler to become a 'milkaholic'. Water should be the only drink offered at mealtimes to encourage eating.

# BREAKFAST

By now, toddlers should be eating the same meals as the rest of the family, albeit in smaller portions. Scatter blueberries over hotcakes, muesli or porridge for an antioxidant hit, necessary for a healthy immune system.

## breakfast hotcakes

1½ cups (225g) self-raising flour

¼ cup (55g) caster (superfine) sugar

1 egg

1¼ cups (310ml) milk

**1** Sift flour and sugar into a medium bowl; whisk in combined egg and milk until smooth. Transfer to a medium jug.
**2** Heat a lightly greased large frying pan over medium heat. Pour ⅓-cup of batter into the pan; cook hotcake until bubbles appear on the surface. Turn hotcake; cook until browned lightly underneath. Remove from pan; repeat with remaining batter.

**prep + cook time** 20 minutes  **makes** 8

tip Many foods go well with hotcakes – serve them with maple syrup and butter, a sprinkle of sugar and lemon juice, or a side order of crispy bacon, if you like. If you add a pinch of bicarbonate of soda to the flour, it will give the hotcakes a light, spongy texture.

cheesy scrambled eggs with spinach

peach bircher muesli

# cheesy scrambled eggs with spinach

50g (1½ ounces) baby spinach leaves

8 eggs

⅓ cup (80g) spreadable cream cheese

1 Coarsely chop spinach.
2 Whisk eggs in a medium bowl until combined, then whisk in cheese and spinach.
3 Heat an oiled large frying pan over low heat. Pour mixture into pan; stir gently until almost set. Serve with toast, if you like.

**prep + cook time** 10 minutes  **serves** 4
**tips** Eggs are a nutritional powerhouse, so they are a great breakfast for growing kids.

# peach bircher muesli

*Start this recipe the evening before as it needs to be refrigerated overnight.*

2 cups (220g) natural muesli

1⅓ cups (330ml) apple juice

¾ cup (210g) greek-style yoghurt

1¼ cups (185g) dried peaches, chopped coarsely

2 tablespoons honey

¾ cup (180ml) milk

1 medium pear (230g), peeled, grated

1 large peach (220g), cut into wedges

¼ cup (20g) toasted shredded coconut

1 Combine muesli, juice, yoghurt, dried peach, honey and milk in a large bowl. Cover; refrigerate overnight.
2 Stir pear into muesli mixture; serve topped with peach wedges and sprinkled with coconut.

**prep time** 25 minutes (+ refrigeration)  **serves** 4
**tips** Store muesli, covered, in the fridge for up to 2 days.
If peaches or pears are out of season use the canned variety.

# zucchini, carrot and cheese omelettes

8 eggs

1 medium zucchini (120g), grated coarsely

1 large carrot (180g), grated coarsely

½ cup (60g) coarsely grated reduced-fat cheddar

1 Whisk eggs in a medium bowl until combined.

2 Pour a quarter of the egg mixture into a heated oiled small frying pan; cook, over medium heat, until omelette is almost set. Sprinkle a quarter of the zucchini, carrot and cheese over half of the omelette. Fold omelette in half, continue cooking until the cheese melts. Slide omelette onto plate; cover to keep warm.

3 Repeat process with remaining ingredients to make 3 more omelettes. Chop omelette into bite size pieces for your toddler.

**prep + cook time** 30 minutes **serves** 4
**serving suggestion** Toasted turkish bread.

tip A quick and easy before pre-school tummy-filler. Add a bit of crisp bacon or even a few pan-fried mushrooms to the omelette, if you like.

porridge with pear compote

strawberry soy smoothie

# porridge with pear compote

3½ cups (875ml) hot water

1½ cups (135g) rolled oats

½ cup (125ml) milk

1 small pear (180g), peeled, cored, chopped coarsely

½ cup (125ml) water

2 tablespoons blueberries

1 Combine the hot water and oats in a medium saucepan over medium heat; cook, stirring, for 5 minutes or until porridge is thick and creamy. Stir in milk.
2 Meanwhile, place pear and the water in a small saucepan; bring to the boil. Reduce heat, simmer, uncovered, for 5 minutes or until soft.
3 Serve porridge topped with pear and 1 tablespoon of the poaching liquid; sprinkle with berries.

**prep + cook time** 20 minutes  **serves** 4

# strawberry soy smoothie

*This recipe is dairy- and egg-free. You can substitute dairy products for the soy and plain ice-cream for the egg-free soy, if there are no dairy- or egg- allergies in the family.*

8 strawberries (160g)

½ cup (125ml) chilled soy milk (see tip)

½ cup (125ml) egg-free vanilla soy ice-cream (see tip)

1 Hull and halve strawberries.
2 Blend or process ingredients until smooth.
3 Pour into glass; serve immediately.

**prep time** 10 minutes  **makes** 1 cup (250ml)
**tip** Always check the labels of soy products carefully for any unexpected allergens.

# waffles with maple syrup

*This recipe is gluten-, wheat-, dairy- and nut-free; the waffles taste yummy, so allergy-free family members can enjoy them as well. You need a waffle iron to cook the waffles.*

200g (6½ ounces) dairy-free spread

¾ cup (165g) caster (superfine) sugar

1 teaspoon vanilla extract

3 eggs, separated

1¼ cups (185g) potato flour

1 cup (160g) brown rice flour

1 teaspoon gluten-free baking powder

1 cup (250ml) water

cooking-oil spray

2 teaspoons pure icing (confectioners') sugar

1 cup (250ml) pure maple syrup

**1** Beat spread, caster sugar and extract in a medium bowl with an electric mixer until light and fluffy. Beat in egg yolks one at a time.

**2** Beat egg whites in a small bowl with an electric mixer until soft peaks form; gently fold into egg-yolk mixture.

**3** Fold sifted dry ingredients and the water into the egg mixture. Do not overmix. Mixture may look slightly curdled at this stage.

**4** Spray a heated waffle iron with cooking oil; pour ½ cup batter over the bottom element of the waffle iron. Close iron; cook waffle about 3 minutes or until browned both sides and crisp. Transfer waffle to plate; cover to keep warm. Repeat with cooking oil and remaining batter.

**5** Dust waffles with sifted icing sugar and serve with syrup.

**prep + cook time** 45 minutes  **makes** 8

**tip** Waffles can be frozen in an airtight container for up to 3 months. Reheat waffles in the oven. Serve waffles with your favourite toppings.

# LUNCH

Sandwiches and finger foods are great for lunch, but make sure they're eaten at the table. Don't allow your toddler to wander around while eating; at this stage they should be encouraged to focus on the job at hand.

## chicken and tomato toasted tortillas

2 medium tomatoes (300g), chopped finely

1 cup (160g) coarsely chopped barbecued chicken

4 large flour tortillas (230g)

1 cup (120g) coarsely grated cheddar

**1** Preheat sandwich press.

**2** Combine tomato and chicken in a medium bowl. Divide mixture between tortillas; top with cheese. Fold over to enclose filling.

**3** Toast in sandwich press until golden brown. Cut into bite-sized pieces for your child.

**prep + cook time** 20 minutes  **makes** 4

**tips**  Add refried beans, avocado and a handful of fresh salad leaves to transform this lunch into a healthy dinner for older toddlers. Cans of refried beans can be found in your local supermarket in the Mexican section. If you don't have a sandwich press, heat a large frying pan over medium heat; cook tortillas until golden on both sides and cheese is melted.

# ricotta and honey sandwiches with dried pears

½ cup (100g) ricotta

1 tablespoon honey

¼ cup (35g) dried pears, chopped finely

6 slices raisin bread

1 Combine ricotta, honey and pear in a small bowl.

2 Spread ricotta mixture over three bread slices; top with remaining bread slices. Discard crusts; cut sandwiches into squares.

**prep time** 10 minutes  **makes** 12

**tip**  You can substitute dried apricots or apple rings for the dried pears, if you like.

# turkey on toasted turkish bread

1 small turkish bread roll (160g)

1 tablespoon cranberry sauce

30g (1 ounce) shaved turkey

10g (½ ounce) shaved jarlsberg cheese

10g (½ ounce) baby spinach leaves

**1** Preheat sandwich press.

**2** Split bread roll in half; spread sauce on cut sides then sandwich turkey, cheese and spinach between pieces.

**3** Toast in sandwich press until golden brown.

**prep + cook time** 10 minutes  **makes** 1

**tips**  Cut sandwich into bite-sizes pieces for your child before serving. This filling is great on sliced bread as a sandwich.

You need to soak 24 ice-block sticks or bamboo skewers in cold water for at least 30 minutes to prevent them from scorching during cooking; or you can wrap the ends in foil. Kofta can be made and shaped onto the sticks a day ahead; keep, covered, in the fridge. Uncooked kofta can be frozen for up to two months; thaw them in the fridge the night before you need them.

# lamb kofta sticks

500g (1 pound) minced (ground) lamb

1 egg

1 small brown onion (80g), chopped finely

2 tablespoons finely chopped fresh flat-leaf parsley

**1** Combine lamb, egg, onion and parsley in a medium bowl.
**2** Shape level tablespoons of lamb mixture into sausage shapes on 24 ice-block sticks; flatten mixture slightly.
**3** Cook kofta sticks, in batches, in a heated oiled large frying pan, over medium heat, until cooked through.

**prep + cook time** 35 minutes  **makes** 24
**serving suggestion**  Accompany with yoghurt for dipping, if you like.

vegetable cakes

broccoli and cheese frittata

# vegetable cakes

¼ cup (60g) coarsely grated potato

2 tablespoons finely chopped red capsicum (bell pepper)

2 tablespoons finely chopped button mushrooms

2 eggs, beaten lightly

**1** Heat a lightly oiled large frying pan; cook potato, capsicum and mushroom, stirring, over medium heat until tender. Cool for 10 minutes.
**2** Combine potato mixture in a small bowl with egg.
**3** Wipe frying pan clean with absorbent paper. Lightly oil the pan and heat over a low heat; place four oiled egg rings into pan. Divide potato mixture into rings; cook for 5 minutes.
**4** Using egg slide, turn vegetable cakes over; cook until cakes are set.

**prep + cook time** 25 minutes  **makes** 4

**tip** These are quick and easy to make. Use any vegetables you like, but be sure to grate any hard root vegetables. Double or triple the recipe to fed the family, and refrigerate any remainders for lunch the next day. Adults could pack leftovers to take as a work lunch.

# broccoli and cheese frittata

400g (12½ ounces) broccoli, sliced thinly

1 cup (120g) coarsely grated cheddar

7 eggs

⅓ cup (80ml) pouring cream

**1** Preheat oven to 180°C/350°F. Grease 20cm x 30cm (8-inch x 12-inch) lamington pan. Line base and sides with baking paper.
**2** Place broccoli in a large saucepan of boiling water; return to the boil, drain. Rinse under cold water; drain. Pat dry with absorbent paper.
**3** Layer broccoli and cheese in pan then pour over combined eggs and cream. Bake, uncovered, for 25 minutes or until frittata sets. Cool for 5 minutes before cutting into squares.

**prep + cook time** 45 minutes  **serves** 4

**tip** Broccoli is a great vegetable for kids to eat: it provides them with a good source of dietary fibre, as well as potassium, vitamin E, folate and beta carotene.

# sweet corn and tuna sandwich

½ x 185g (6-ounce) can tuna in springwater

2 tablespoons rinsed, drained canned sweet corn kernels

1 tablespoon mayonnaise

2 slices multigrain bread (90g)

¼ lebanese cucumber (30g), sliced thinly

1 Combine the tuna, corn and mayonnaise in a small bowl.
2 Spread mixture onto one slice of bread. Top with cucumber and another slice of bread. Cut into squares or triangles.

**prep time** 10 minutes  **serves** 1

# beef, cheese and carrot sandwich

½ small carrot (70g), grated coarsely

2 tablespoons spreadable cream cheese

2 tablespoons finely shredded iceberg lettuce

2 slices white bread (90g)

¼ cup finely chopped roast beef

1 Combine carrot, cheese and lettuce in a small bowl.
2 Spread half the carrot mixture on one slice of bread; top with beef, remaining carrot mixture and another slice of bread. Cut into squares or triangles.

**prep time** 10 minutes  **serves** 1

sweet corn and tuna sandwich

beef, cheese and carrot sandwich

Playtime is essential for toddlers – it increases their muscle tone, enhances their motor skills (coordination) and develops their bone strength (density).

# lentil patties

¼ cup (50g) red lentils

1 medium potato (200g), chopped coarsely

¼ cup (30g) frozen peas

½ small carrot (35g), grated coarsely

½ small brown onion (40g), grated finely

½ cup (50g) packaged breadcrumbs

**1** Cook lentils in a small saucepan of boiling water for 10 minutes or until tender; drain.

**2** Meanwhile, boil, steam or microwave potato and peas, separately, until tender; drain. Mash potato and peas in a medium bowl.

**3** Add lentils, carrot, onion and half the breadcrumbs to potato mixture; mix to combine. Using your hand, shape the mixture into 12 patties.

**4** Coat patties with remaining breadcrumbs; cook patties, uncovered, in a large heated lightly oiled frying pan, over low heat, for 10 minutes or until patties are browned both sides and heated through.

**prep + cook time** 40 minutes  **makes** 12

**tip** Store patties, covered, in the fridge for up to 2 days. Freeze uncooked patties for up to 1 month. Defrost patties in the fridge before cooking.

# DINNER

Add interest to your toddler's mealtime by using different shapes cut from vegetables or bread (stars and small gingerbread men are good). A variety of vegetables not only adds colour, but also adds a wide array of vitamins and minerals. Most of these recipes serve a family of 4.

## chunky beef and vegetable soup

2 tablespoons olive oil

600g (1¼ pounds) gravy beef with the fat cut off, chopped coarsely

1 medium brown onion (150g), chopped coarsely

1 clove garlic, crushed

1.5 litres (6 cups) water

1 cup (250ml) beef stock

400g (12½ ounces) canned diced tomatoes

2 stalks celery (300g), trimmed, chopped coarsely

1 medium carrot (120g), chopped coarsely

2 small potatoes (240g), chopped coarsely

1 cup (120g) frozen peas and corn mix

**1** Heat half the oil in a large saucepan over high heat; cook beef, in batches, stirring, for 3 minutes or until brown. Remove from pan.

**2** Heat remaining oil in pan; cook onion and garlic; stirring, for 3 minutes or until onion is soft. Return beef to pan with the water, stock and tomatoes; bring to the boil. Reduce heat to low, simmer, covered, for 1½ hours, skimming the fat off the surface of the soup occasionally

**3** Add celery, carrot and potato to the soup. Simmer for 20 minutes or until the vegetables are tender.

**4** Add peas and corn; stir, until heated through. Serve soup sprinkled with some flat-leaf parsley leaves, if you like.

**prep + cook time** 2½ hours  **serves** 4

**tip**  If you would like to add more vegetables, trim 1 bunch spinach, coarsely chop the leaves and toss them into the soup when you add the peas and corn. Omit the potatoes if you would like to freeze the soup, as potato turns watery on thawing. Freeze in individual portions for up to 2 months.

Serve the soup with star-shaped
wholemeal toasts. Use star-shaped
cookie cutters to cut out the stars
and toast them, both sides, under
a preheated grill (or broiler).

# sang choy bow

2 teaspoons sesame oil

1 small brown onion (80g), chopped finely

2 cloves garlic, crushed

2 teaspoons grated fresh ginger

500g (1 pound) minced (ground) pork

2 tablespoons water

125g (4 ounces) fresh shiitake mushrooms,
chopped finely

2 tablespoons light soy sauce

2 tablespoons oyster sauce

1 tablespoon lime juice

2 cups (160g) bean sprouts

4 green onions (scallions), sliced thinly

¼ cup coarsely chopped fresh coriander (cilantro)

12 large iceberg lettuce leaves, with white parts cut off

1 Heat oil in a wok over medium-high heat; stir-fry brown onion, garlic and ginger for 2 minutes or until the onion is soft. Add pork; stir-fry for 5 minutes or until pork is browned.
2 Add the water, mushrooms, sauces and juice; stir-fry for 2 minutes or until mushrooms are tender. Remove wok from heat. Stir in sprouts, green onion and coriander.
3 Arrange lettuce leaves on a large platter. Spoon the pork mixture into the lettuce leaf 'cups'.

**prep + cook time** 40 minutes  **serves** 4
**tips**  Swap shiitake mushrooms for button mushrooms, if you prefer.

# savoury vegetable mince

1 medium brown onion (150g), chopped finely

600g (1¼ pounds) minced (ground) beef

800g (1½ pounds) canned diced tomatoes

1 cup (150g) frozen mixed vegetables

**1** Cook onion in a heated oiled large saucepan, over high heat, stirring, for 3 minutes or until softened. Add beef; cook, stirring, for 5 minutes or until beef changes colour.
**2** Add tomatoes to pan; bring to the boil. Simmer, uncovered, stirring occasionally, for 15 minutes or until mixture is thick. Add vegetables, simmer for a further 5 minutes or until vegetables are heated through.

**prep + cook time** 40 minutes **serves** 4

**tip** Savoury mince on toast is an all-time family favourite; kids and adults of all ages love it. Serve on buttered toast or, to extend the meal even further, mix the mince with cooked pasta. You can use any vegetables you like in this recipe. Freeze ¼ cups of savoury mince, in an airtight container, for up to 1 month.

# sausage pasta bake

6 thick beef sausages (480g)

375g (12 ounces) penne

1 tablespoon olive oil

1 medium brown onion (150g), chopped coarsely

1 small red capsicum (bell peppers) (150g), chopped coarsely

1 small yellow capsicum (bell peppers) (150g), chopped coarsely

1 large zucchini (150g), sliced thinly

200g (6½ ounces) button mushrooms, quartered

¼ cup loosely packed coarsely chopped fresh basil

700g (1½ ounces) bottled low-salt tomato pasta sauce

1 cup (100g) coarsely grated mozzarella

½ cup (40g) coarsely grated parmesan

**1** Preheat oven to 200°C/400°F.
**2** Cook sausages in a heated oiled large frying pan over medium-high heat until cooked through; cut into 1cm (½-inch) slices.
**3** Meanwhile, cook pasta in a large saucepan of boiling water until just tender; drain.
**4** Heat oil in same cleaned frying pan over high heat; cook onion, capsicum and zucchini, stirring, for 4 minutes or until vegetables are tender. Add mushrooms, basil and pasta sauce; bring to the boil. Reduce heat; simmer for 5 minutes.
**5** Combine pasta in a large bowl with sliced sausage, vegetable mixture and half the mozzarella.
**6** Place mixture in a 2.5-litre (10-cup) shallow baking dish; sprinkle with combined remaining cheeses. Bake, uncovered, for 25 minutes or until browned lightly.

**prep + cook time** 1 hour **serves** 6

**tip** Chop your toddler's portion of the bake into small bite-sized pieces.

savoury vegetable mince

sausage pasta bake

# fish fingers with coleslaw

1kg (2 pounds) white fish fillets, skin and bones removed, chopped coarsely

2 tablespoons coarsely chopped fresh chives

2 egg whites

1¼ cups (125g) packaged breadcrumbs

2 tablespoons olive oil

coleslaw

1½ cups (120g) finely shredded red cabbage

1 cup (80g) finely shredded savoy cabbage

1 medium carrot (120g), grated coarsely

2 tablespoons coarsely chopped fresh flat-leaf parsley

1 green onion (scallion), sliced thinly

2 tablespoons mayonnaise

1 tablespoon sour cream

1 tablespoon white wine vinegar

1 Make coleslaw.

2 Grease 20cm x 30cm (8-inch x 12-inch) rectangular pan.

3 Blend or process fish and chives until smooth. Press mixture evenly into pan, turn out onto a baking-paper-lined tray; cut into eight 20cm (8-inch) slices; cut each slice in half to make 16 fish fingers.

4 Whisk egg whites lightly in a medium shallow bowl; place breadcrumbs in another medium shallow bowl. Dip fish fingers into egg whites, then in breadcrumbs to coat. Heat oil in a large frying pan over medium-high heat; cook fish fingers, in batches, for 3 minutes or until browned lightly and cooked through. Drain on absorbent paper. Cut fish fingers into bite-sized pieces for toddlers.

5 Serve fish fingers with coleslaw; season to taste.

coleslaw Combine ingredients in a large bowl.

prep + cook time 35 minutes serves 4

tips We used ling fillets in this recipe, but any white fish fillets will do. Accompany the fish fingers with oven-baked potato wedges and a squeeze of lemon, if you like. Fish fingers can be crumbed, placed on a tray in a single layer, covered, then refrigerated for several hours ahead of cooking. Coleslaw can be made and refrigerated up to 3 hours ahead of serving time.

# chicken with avocado and tomato salsa

4 chicken breast fillets (800g)

salsa

1 medium avocado (250g), chopped finely

2 medium tomatoes (300g), chopped finely

2 tablespoons lime juice

**1** Make salsa.
**2** Cook chicken in a heated oiled large frying pan, over medium heat, for 4 minutes each side or until cooked through. When cool enough to handle, slice chicken; serve with salsa.
**salsa** Combine avocado, tomato and juice in a medium bowl.

**prep + cook time** 20 minutes **serves** 4
**tips** Chop chicken into bite-sized pieces for younger toddlers. Adults can add chopped red onion, coriander (cilantro) and capsicum to the salsa for extra colour and flavour. Accompany with flat bread, if you like.

# meatballs in tomato sauce

750g (1½ pounds) beef sausages

250g (8 ounces) cherry tomatoes, halved

400g (13 ounces) bottled low-salt tomato pasta sauce

¼ cup loosely packed fresh basil leaves

**1** Squeeze meat from sausages; roll tablespoons of the meat into balls.
**2** Cook meatballs, in a heated oiled large frying pan, in batches, over high heat, for 5 minutes or until browned. Add tomatoes, sauce and half the basil. Bring to the boil; simmer, uncovered, for 5 minutes or until meatballs are cooked through.
**3** Serve meatballs sprinkled with remaining basil.

**prep + cook time** 25 minutes **serves** 4
**tips** Use flavoured sausages instead of plain. If you prefer, cook the sausages whole then slice them thickly and add to the tomato mixture. Cut meatballs into smaller pieces for younger toddlers. Freeze ¼ cups of chopped meatballs with sauce, in an airtight container, for up to 1 month.
**serving suggestion** Spaghetti and some grated parmesan.

chicken with avocado and tomato salsa

meatballs in tomato sauce

## mini pineapple and carrot cakes

Preheat oven to 180°C/350°F. Grease 18 holes of two 12-hole (1-tablespoon/20ml) mini muffin pans. Sift ⅓ cup (50g) plain (all-purpose) flour, ½ cup (75g) self-raising flour, ½ teaspoon bicarbonate of soda (baking soda), ¼ cup (55g) caster (superfine) sugar and ½ teaspoon ground cinnamon into a medium bowl. Add ½ x 450g (14½-ounce) can drained crushed pineapple and ⅔ cup (160g) firmly packed finely grated carrot; stir in combined ⅓ cup vegetable oil and 1 lightly beaten egg (do not over-mix). Divide mixture into pan holes. Bake for 15 minutes. Stand muffins in pans for 5 minutes before turning, top-side up, onto wire racks to cool. To make cream cheese frosting: combine 125g (4 ounces) softened cream cheese, 1 tablespoon sifted icing (confectioners') sugar, 1 teaspoon lemon juice and 2 teaspoons milk in a small bowl. Spread cooled muffins with icing.

**prep + cook time** 50 minutes (+ cooling)  **makes** 18
**tip** Un-iced cakes are suitable to freeze for up to 3 months.

## cheesy pumpkin scones

Preheat oven to 240°C/475°F. Grease a deep 19cm (8-inch) square cake pan. Coarsely chop 250g (8 ounce) pumpkin; boil, steam or microwave pumpkin until just tender; drain. Mash pumpkin in a small bowl; cool 10 minutes. Coarsely chop 50g (1½ ounce) butter. Place 2½ cups (375g) self-raising flour and 1 tablespoon caster (superfine) sugar in a medium bowl; use fingertips to rub in butter until mixture resembles breadcrumbs. Stir in ¼ cup (30g) coarsely grated cheddar, ¼ cup (20g) coarsely grated parmesan and the mashed pumpkin. Make a well in the centre of the mixture; add only enough milk to mix to a soft, sticky dough (you'll need approximately ½ cup milk). Turn dough onto a lightly floured surface; knead lightly until smooth. Press dough out into a 2cm (¾-inch) thickness; cut 16 x 4.5cm (1¾-inch) rounds from dough. Place scones, side by side just touching, in prepared pan; sprinkle with an extra ¼ cup (20g) coarsely grated parmesan. Bake, uncovered, for 20 minutes.

**prep + cook time** 45 minutes (+ cooling)  **makes** 16
tips  Scones are suitable to freeze for up to 2 months. Defrost in a microwave oven on medium (50% ) in 30 second bursts until just warm.

## melon and ham wrap

Cut half a peeled small rockmelon (650g) lengthways into eight wedges; cut each wedge in half crossways. Wrap a piece of thinly sliced or shaved ham around each rockmelon piece.

**prep time** 10 minutes
**tip** This is a great afternoon snack. You'll need about 160g (5 ounces) ham.

## carrot dip

Coarsely chop 5 medium carrots (600g). Boil, steam or microwave carrot until tender; drain. Heat 1 tablespoon olive oil in a large frying pan over medium heat; cook 1 crushed garlic clove and ½ teaspoon ground cumin, stirring, for 30 seconds or until fragrant. Stir in carrot and 2 teaspoons lemon juice; cook, stirring, until combined. Remove from heat; cool 10 minutes. Blend or process carrot mixture with ⅓ cup plain yoghurt until just smooth. Serve carrot dip with grissini sticks, if you like.

**prep + cook time** 35 minutes (+ cooling)
**makes** 1½ cups (18 tablespoons)
**tips** The dip can be stored, covered, in the fridge for up to 3 days. Serve with blanched vegetables such as snow peas, baby corn, red capsicum (bell peppers).

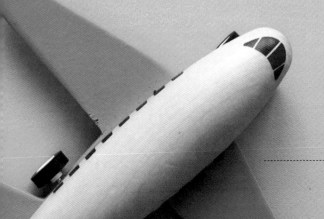

# chicken vegetable soup with croûtons

1 tablespoon olive oil

1 medium brown onion (150g), chopped finely

1 clove garlic, crushed

2 medium tomatoes (300g), chopped finely

400g (12½ ounces) chicken breast fillets, sliced thinly

450g (14½ ounces) finely chopped pumpkin

2 litres (8 cups) salt-reduced chicken stock

2 slices wholemeal bread (90g)

420g (13½ ounces) canned borlotti beans, rinsed, drained

150g (4½ ounces) broccoli, cut into florets

½ cup (40g) coarsely grated parmesan

1 Heat half the oil in a large saucepan over medium-high heat; cook onion, garlic and tomato, stirring, for 4 minutes or until onion softens. Add chicken, pumpkin and stock; bring to the boil. Reduce heat; simmer, uncovered, for 10 minutes or until pumpkin is almost tender.

2 Meanwhile, preheat grill (broiler).

3 Cut bread into shapes using a small round cutter (or cut into small cubes); combine bread and remaining oil in a small bowl. Place bread, in a single layer, on an oven tray; toast, under grill, until croûtons are crisp and golden.

4 Add beans and broccoli to soup; cook for 3 minutes or until heated through.

5 Serve soup topped with croûtons and sprinkled with cheese.

**prep + cook** 45 minutes  **serves** 6

**tip**  Soup is suitable to freeze. To make this soup more fun for toddlers cut different shapes from bread like stars, hearts or animals. You could get older toddlers to cut the shapes from the bread to get them involved in the preparation of the meal.

# creamy tuna pasta bake

375g (12 ounces) macaroni pasta

600ml pouring cream

1½ cups (180g) coarsely grated cheddar

425g (13½ ounces) canned tuna in springwater, drained, flaked

1 Cook pasta in a large saucepan of boiling water until tender; drain well.

2 Bring cream to the boil in same pan. Reduce heat; stir in pasta, half the cheese and all the tuna. Stir over heat until mixture comes to the boil.

3 Meanwhile, preheat grill (broiler).

4 Spoon pasta into a shallow 2-litre (8-cup) baking dish. Sprinkle with remaining cheese; place under grill until cheese melts and is browned lightly.

**prep + cook time** 25 minutes **serves** 4

**tip** This recipe also works well with canned salmon.

# beef & broccolini stir-fry

2 teaspoons olive oil

625g (1¼ pounds) beef rump steak, sliced thinly

350g (11 ounces) broccolini, chopped coarsely

2 tablespoons water

2 tablespoons sweet chilli sauce

¼ cup (60ml) oyster sauce

1 Heat oil in a wok over high heat; stir-fry beef, in batches, until browned all over. Remove from wok.

2 Stir-fry broccolini with the water in wok until tender.

3 Return beef to wok with sauces. Stir-fry until heated through.

**prep + cook time** 20 minutes **serves** 4

**tip** Broccolini is milder and sweeter than traditional broccoli and it is edible from flower to stem. When buying broccolini look for shiny stems with dark green buds and leaves.

**serving suggestion** Steamed rice or stir-fried rice noodles.

creamy tuna pasta bake

beef and broccolini stir-fry

tip Cutlets are great for toddlers as they can pick them up and feed themselves. For younger toddlers you might like to remove the meat from the bone and chop into bite-sized pieces; serve the bone as well and allow them to chew any remaining meat off the bone. If feeding adults, you may need to increase the number of cutlets, and add other vegetables, such as steamed carrots and beans. You can use fresh peas instead of frozen peas if they are in season. You will need approximately 1kg of fresh peas to get 500g of shelled peas. When shopping for peas, look for bright green pods. You want them to look full but not swollen. Avoid pods that are discoloured, wrinkly, dry or split.

# lamb cutlets with pea mash

500g (1 pound) frozen green peas

30g (1 ounce) butter

¼ cup (60ml) water

1 tablespoon finely chopped fresh mint

8 lamb cutlets (600g)

1 Heat a medium saucepan over high heat; cook peas, butter and the water, stirring, until butter melts and peas are hot. Process pea mixture until almost smooth; stir through mint, season to taste.
2 Meanwhile, cook lamb in a heated oiled large frying pan, over medium-high heat, until cooked as desired.
3 Serve lamb with pea mash.

**prep + cook time** 30 minutes  **serves** 4

# PARTY FOOD

The recipes in this section are all gluten-free, to help parents cater for children with wheat intolerance or allergies. They are recipes everyone can enjoy, so you don't have to make separate food for your child or children with allergies.

## dainty cupcakes

*These cupcakes are gluten-, wheat- and nut-free.*

200g (6½ ounces) butter

2¼ cups (300g) gluten-free self-raising flour

1 cup (220g) caster (superfine) sugar

½ cup (125ml) milk

2 eggs

2 egg whites

24 gluten-free edible sugar flowers

butter cream

125g (4 ounces) butter

1½ cups (240g) pure icing (confectioners') sugar

2 tablespoons milk

**1** Preheat oven to 180°C/350°F.

**2** Line 20 holes of two 12-hole (⅓-cup/80ml) muffin pans with paper cases.

**3** Beat butter in a medium bowl with an electric mixer until pale. Sift flours with ¼ cup of the sugar. Add half the flour-sugar mixture and half the milk to the butter; beat until combined. Add remaining flour-sugar mixture and milk; beat until mixture is well combined.

**4** Place eggs and egg whites in a small bowl; beat with an electric mixer on high speed until eggs are thick and creamy. Add remaining sugar, a little at a time; beating until sugar has dissolved between each addition. Gradually add egg mixture, a little at a time, to flour mixture; beating until the mixture is well combined.

**5** Spoon mixture into paper cases. Bake for 20 minutes. Stand cakes in pans for 5 minutes before turning, top-side up, onto wire racks to cool.

**6** Meanwhile, make butter cream.

**7** Spread cooled cakes with butter cream; decorate with flowers.

**butter cream** Beat butter in a small bowl with an electric mixer until very pale. Add half the sifted icing sugar and half the milk; beat until well combined. Add remaining sifted icing sugar and the milk; beat until mixture is smooth.

**prep + cook time** 1½ hours (+ cooling) **makes** 20
**tip** Un-iced cakes can be frozen up to 3 months. If you like, use a small heart-shaped cutter to dust heart shapes over the top of the cakes with sifted icing sugar.

passionfruit kisses

fruit skewers

# passionfruit kisses

*This recipe is gluten-, dairy-, wheat- and nut-free.*

3 eggs

½ cup (110g) caster (superfine) sugar

¾ cup (110g) (100% corn) cornflour (cornstarch)

2 tablespoons pure icing (confectioners') sugar

passionfruit filling

90g (3 ounces) dairy-free spread

1½ cups (240g) pure icing (confectioners') sugar

2 tablespoons passionfruit pulp

1 Preheat oven to 180°C/350°F. Grease two 12-hole
(1½-tablespoon/30ml) round-based patty pans.
2 Beat eggs in a small bowl with an electric mixer until thick
and creamy. Add sugar, one tablespoon at a time, beating
until sugar dissolves between additions. Gently fold in the
triple-sifted cornflour. Drop one level tablespoon of mixture
into each pan hole.
3 Bake cakes about 10 minutes. Turn cakes immediately onto
baking-paper-covered wire racks by tapping pans upside-
down firmly on the bench to release the cakes; cool.
4 Meanwhile, make passionfruit filling.
5 Sandwich cold kisses with passionfruit filling; serve dusted
with sifted icing sugar.
**passionfruit filling** Beat spread in a small bowl with an
electric mixer until as white as possible; gradually beat in
sifted icing sugar. Stir in passionfruit.

**prep + cook time** 40 minutes (+ cooling)
**makes** 12 sandwiched kisses (24 single cakes)
**tip** Kisses can be stored in an airtight container for 1 day.
Unfilled kisses can be frozen for up to 3 months.

# fruit skewers

*This recipe is gluten-, dairy-, wheat-, egg- and nut-free.*

2 large kiwifruit (240g)

2 medium oranges (500g)

¼ seedless watermelon (1.5kg)

4 strawberries (48g)

1 Peel the kiwifruit and oranges. Remove rind from the melon,
then cut all fruit into slices.
2 Use various sizes of star cutters and a moon cutter to cut out
shapes from fruit.
3 Thread fruit onto 8 bamboo skewers.

**prep time** 20 minutes  **makes** 8
**tips**  You can use whatever fruit you like. Leftover fruit pieces
can be used in juices or smoothies.

# mini meat pies

*These little pies are gluten-, wheat- and nut-free.*
*You need 24 x ¼-cup (60ml) foil pie cases with 7cm (2¾-inch)*
*diameter tops and 5cm (2-inch) diameter bases; and a 9cm*
*(3¾-inch) and 7cm (2¾-inch) round cutter.*

2 teaspoons vegetable oil

1 medium brown onion (150g), chopped finely

2 gluten-free rindless bacon slices (130g), chopped finely

350g (11 ounces) minced (ground) beef

2 tablespoons tomato paste

¼ cup (35g) arrowroot

2 cups (500ml) gluten-free beef stock

1 egg, beaten lightly

pastry

400g (12½ ounces) cold butter, chopped coarsely

3½ cups (630g) rice flour

⅔ cup (100g) (100% corn) cornflour (cornstarch)

⅔ cup (80g) soy flour

½ cup (125ml) iced water, approximately

**1** Heat oil in a medium saucepan over medium-high heat; cook onion and bacon, stirring, for 4 minutes or until onion softens and bacon is browned. Add beef; cook, stirring, for 5 minutes or until browned.

**2** Add paste and combined arrowroot and stock to pan; bring to the boil, stirring. Reduce heat; simmer, uncovered, until thickened. Cool.

**3** Meanwhile, make pastry.

**4** Preheat oven to 220°C/425°F. Oil 24 x ¼-cup (60ml) foil pie cases with 7cm (2¾-inch) diameter tops, 5cm (2-inch) diameter bases; place on oven tray.

**5** Roll pastry between sheets of baking paper until 5mm (¼ inch) thick; cut 24 x 9cm (3¾-inch) rounds from pastry. Ease pastry rounds into foil cases; press into base and sides. Spoon beef mixture into pastry cases. Brush edges with egg. Cut 24 x 7cm (2¾-inch) rounds from remaining pastry; place rounds on pies, press to seal edges. Brush pies with egg. Refrigerate pies for 1 hour. Make two small cuts into the top of each pie.

**6** Bake pies about 25 minutes or until filling is heated through and pastry is lightly golden. Serve with gluten-free tomato sauce, if you like.

**pastry** Process butter and flours until mixture is fine. Add enough of the water to make ingredients come together. Cover; refrigerate 30 minutes.

**prep + cook time** 1 hour (+ refrigeration) **makes** 24
**tip** Pies can be made ahead and frozen for up to 1 month. Reheat from frozen in a preheated 160°C/325°F oven. Cover with foil if pastry is over-browning.

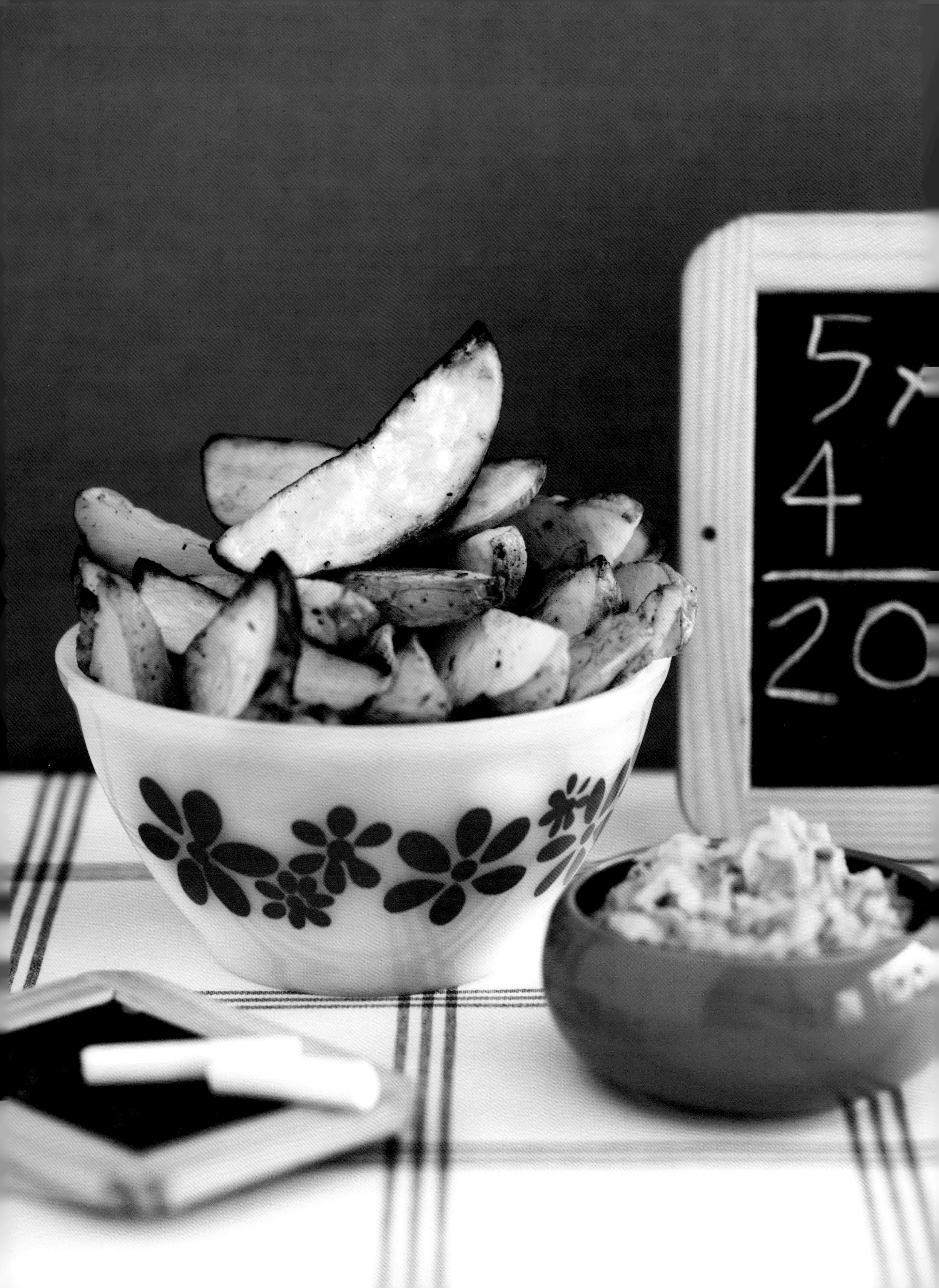
5×
4
20

# potato wedges with guacamole

*This recipe is dairy-, egg- and nut- free.*

4 medium potatoes (800g)

1 tablespoon olive oil

1 tablespoon chicken seasoning

guacamole

3 medium avocados (750g)

½ small red onion (50g), chopped finely

1 small roma (egg) tomato (60g), seeded, chopped finely

1 tablespoon lime juice

¼ cup finely chopped fresh coriander (cilantro)

1 Preheat oven to 240°C/475°F.

2 Wash and scrub potatoes well to remove any dirt from skin; pat dry with absorbent paper.

3 Cut unpeeled potatoes in half; cut each half into wedges. Place wedges in a medium bowl with oil and seasoning; turn to coat in mixture.

4 Place wedges in an oiled baking dish. Bake 40 minutes or until golden brown.

5 Meanwhile, make guacamole.

6 Serve wedges with guacamole.

**guacamole** Mash avocados in a medium bowl. Stir in onion, tomato, juice and coriander.

**prep + cook time** 1 hour **serves** 4

**tip** Guacamole can be made 2 hours ahead, keep, covered, in the fridge. While older children may be happy to eat the wedges with the guacamole, younger toddlers may prefer tomato sauce, instead.

# the 'still really terrific' at two cake

*This recipe is gluten-free. You need a 5cm x 34cm (6-inch x 13½-inch) number 2 cake pan and a 35cm x 45cm (14-inch x 18-inch) rectangular cake board.*

3 x 470g (15-ounce) packets gluten-free vanilla cake mix

⅓ cup (110g) apricot jam (conserve), warmed, strained

900g (1¾ pounds) ready-made white icing

½ cup (80g) pure icing (confectioners') sugar

blue food colouring

**glacé icing**

2 cups (160g) pure icing (confectioners') sugar

1 tablespoon water, approximately

**decorations**

½ cup (2 sachets) gluten-free sprinkles (see tips)

**1** Preheat oven to 180°C/350°F. Grease cake pan; line base with baking paper.

**2** Make cakes according to directions on packets. Spread mixture into pan; bake about 40 minutes. Stand cake in pan 5 minutes before turning, top-side up, onto a wire rack to cool.

**3** Level cake top; position cake on cake board, brush cake all over with warmed jam.

**4** Knead ready-made icing on a surface dusted with sifted icing sugar until icing loses its stickiness; tint pale blue. Roll out half the icing until 5mm (¼-inch) thick. Using rolling pin, lift icing over bottom half of cake. Using sugared hands, mould icing over top and sides of cake; trim neatly around base.

**5** Repeat with remaining icing for top half of cake, carefully joining in the middle.

**6** Make glacé icing. Using picture as a guide, and working quickly, spread glacé icing over cake. Decorate cake with sprinkles immediately, before icing sets.

**glacé icing** Sift icing sugar into a medium heatproof bowl, stir in enough water to give a firm paste. Tint a darker blue than the icing on the cake. Stir the paste over a medium saucepan of hot water (don't let the water touch the base of the bowl) until icing is spreadable; do not overheat. The bottom of the bowl should feel warm (not hot) to the touch. Use immediately.

**prep + cook time** 2 hours (+ cooling) **serves** 18
**tips** We found it easier to cover half the cake at a time with the ready-made icing. This stage can be done up to two days ahead of the party. Complete the cake up to 4 hours ahead. For a completely gluten-free cake, make sure you buy gluten-free sprinkles; they should be free from wheat starch, so check the ingredient list. You can substitute ordinary cake mix for the gluten-free mix, if no one has a gluten allergy. The number 2 cake pan can be hired from cake decorating shops.

# the 'not yet so terrible' threes

*This recipe is gluten-free. You need a 23cm x 34cm (9¼-inch x 13½-inch) number 3 cake pan and a 25cm x 40cm (10-inch x 16-inch) rectangular cake board.*

### cake

3 x 470g (15-ounce) packets gluten-free vanilla cake mix

pink food colouring

### butter cream

250g (8 ounces) butter

3 cups (320g) pure icing (confectioners') sugar

2 tablespoons milk

### decorations

16 white chocolate Melts

**1** Preheat oven to 180°C/350°F. Grease cake pan; line base with baking paper.

**2** Make cakes according to directions on packets. Spread mixture into pan; bake about 40 minutes. Stand cake in pan for 5 minutes before turning, top-side up, onto a wire rack to cool.

**3** Level cake top; turn cake, cut-side down, on cake board.

**4** Make butter cream. Spread all over cake.

**5** Use a small round cutter, or sharp knife, to cut through about half of the Melts, making the edges rounded so they will fit the rounded edges of the cake. Using picture as a guide, decorate cake with Melts.

**butter cream** Beat butter in a small bowl with an electric mixer until as white as possible. Gradually beat in half the sifted icing sugar, milk then remaining icing sugar. Tint butter cream pink.

**prep + cook time** 2 hours (+ cooling)  **serves** 18
**tips** Cake can be made and decorated a day ahead. Store in a cool, dry place. A number 3 cake pan can be hired from cake decorating shops. You can substitute ordinary cake mix for the gluten-free mix, if no one has a gluten allergy.

# 3-5 years

By this stage your child should be enjoying family meals (most of these recipes will feed a family of 4). Sitting down together to eat around the table is one of the most important habits you can build. Impart healthy eating habits - teach by example – and talk to them about the importance of eating good foods. Encourage them to think whether they are hungry above the neck (just feel like eating something nice) or below the neck (tummy rumbling means they really are hungry). Make water the main drink and teach them the difference between occasional and everyday foods. Your child will still need 5-6 meals/snacks a day, but keep to a schedule rather than allowing all-day grazing.

# BREAKFAST

Older children should be in a routine with regards to mealtimes. Breakfast is needed for a big day at school or pre-school, and to give them energy to concentrate and stay active during the day. Kids who are tired tend to have poor concentration and often struggle at school.

## boiled egg with toast soldiers

4 eggs

4 slices white bread (180g)

30g (1 ounce) butter, softened

**1** Place eggs into a medium saucepan; fill saucepan with enough cold water to just cover eggs. Cover pan with a lid. Bring to the boil; remove lid. Boil eggs for 3 minutes for soft boiled. Remove from heat; drain.

**2** Meanwhile, toast the bread. Spread bread with butter, cut crusts off the toast, then cut into four strips ('soldiers').

**3** Serve the eggs in egg cups with toast 'soldiers'.

**prep + cook time** 10 minutes  **serves** 4

# baked eggs with ham and cheese

50g (1½ ounces) shaved ham, chopped coarsely

2 green onions (scallions), chopped finely

4 eggs

⅓ cup (40g) coarsely grated cheddar

**1** Preheat oven to 180°C/350°F. Grease four ½-cup (125ml) shallow ovenproof dishes.

**2** Divide ham and onion among dishes. Break one egg into a small cup, then carefully slide egg from cup over ham and onion in dish. Repeat with remaining eggs. Sprinkle dishes with equal amounts of cheese.

**3** Place dishes on oven tray; bake, uncovered, for 10 minutes or until egg yolk is just set.

**prep + cook time** 20 minutes  **serves** 4

**tips**  Ham can be swapped for bacon. For a vegetarian option swap ham for some sliced mushrooms.

# rolled rice porridge

*This recipe is gluten-, wheat-, yeast-, dairy-, egg-and nut-free.*
*You need to start this recipe the day before.*

1½ cups (160g) rolled rice

1.125 litres (4½ cups) water

⅓ cup (80ml) rice milk

⅓ cup (50g) coarsely chopped dried apricots

¼ cup (10g) flaked coconut, toasted

2 tablespoons honey

**1** Combine rolled rice and 3 cups of the water in a medium bowl. Cover; stand at room temperature overnight.
**2** Place undrained rolled rice in a medium saucepan; cook, stirring, until mixture comes to the boil. Add the remaining water; bring to the boil. Reduce heat; simmer, uncovered, for 5 minutes or until thickened.
**3** Divide porridge and milk among serving bowls. Sprinkle with apricots and coconut; drizzle with honey.

**prep + cook time** 20 minutes (+ standing)  **serves** 4
**tips**  Swap the dried apricots with other dried fruits like figs, dates or cranberries, if you like.

# savoury buckwheat pancakes

*This recipe is gluten-free.*

1 cup (150g) buckwheat flour

½ cup (60g) gluten-free plain (all-purpose) flour

3 teaspoons gluten-free baking powder

2 eggs

2 cups (500ml) buttermilk

50g (1½ ounces) butter, melted

1 small carrot (70g), grated coarsely

1 medium zucchini (120g), grated coarsely

½ cup (80g) fresh or frozen corn kernels

**1** Sift dry ingredients into a large bowl; gradually whisk in combined eggs and buttermilk until smooth. Stir in butter, grated vegetables and corn.

**2** Heat a lightly oiled small frying pan over medium heat, pour ⅓ cup of the batter into pan; cook until bubbles appear on the surface. Turn pancake; cook until browned lightly. Repeat with remaining batter to make a total of 10 pancakes. Serve pancakes topped with spreadable cream cheese and extra corn kernels, if you like.

**prep + cook time** 30 minutes **makes** 10

bran and cranberry muesli

soy pear smoothie

# bran and cranberry muesli

1 cup (90g) rolled oats

¾ cup (55g) all-bran

¼ cup (35g) dried cranberries

2 cups (500ml) milk

1 large banana (230g)

125g (4 ounces) fresh raspberries

1 Combine oats, bran and cranberries in a small bowl to make muesli mixture.

2 Place ⅓ cup muesli in each bowl; top each with ⅓ cup milk.

3 Thinly slice banana. Serve muesli with banana and raspberries.

**prep time** 10 minutes **makes** 6 x ⅓-cup servings

**tip** If you don't want to use dried cranberries, use sultanas or raisins.

# soy pear smoothie

*This recipe is dairy-free.*

2 medium pears (460g)

2 cups (500ml) soy milk

½ teaspoon ground cinnamon

1 tablespoon honey

1 Peel and core pears then chop coarsely.

2 Blend or process ingredients until smooth.

3 Pour into glasses; serve immediately.

**prep time** 5 minutes **serves** 4

**tips** Always check the labels of soy products carefully for any unexpected allergens. If your child does not have a dairy allergy swap the soy milk for full cream milk. You can easily recreate the star shape at home. All you need is a cardboard or plastic star a little bit smaller than the top of the glass. Simply hold the star over the top of the drink and sprinkle the cinnamon accordingly. Get creative with your kids and try other shapes or even letters to add some fun.

# baked beans, bacon, tomato and chives

*This recipe is dairy-, egg-, and nut-free. Use your favourite bread if your family is allergy free.*

420g (13½ ounces) canned baked beans in tomato sauce

4 rindless bacon slices (240g), sliced thinly crossways

4 slices (180g) dairy-free, egg-free, nut-free
multi-grain bread

2 medium tomatoes (300g), chopped coarsely

1 tablespoon finely chopped chives

**1** Preheat grill (broiler).
**2** Heat beans in small saucepan over low heat until heated through.
**3** Meanwhile, cook bacon, in a heated small frying pan, stirring, until crisp; drain on absorbent paper.
**4** Toast bread. Top toast with beans, bacon and tomato; grill about 2 minutes or until hot. Sprinkle with chives.

**prep + cook time** 15 minutes **serves** 4

# LUNCH

Carbohydrates are necessary to refuel tired toddlers, ready for an active afternoon's play. Wholegrain bread, rolls and pasta are low GI, so they keep little tummies feeling fuller for longer. Fresh fruit is a healthy snack.

## chicken schnitzel sandwiches

4 chicken breast fillets (800g)

¼ cup (35g) plain (all-purpose) flour

1 egg

1 tablespoon milk

1 cup (70g) stale breadcrumbs

¼ cup (60ml) olive oil

3 medium red onions (510g), sliced thinly

1 loaf turkish bread (430g), cut into four pieces

⅓ iceberg lettuce (200g), shredded coarsely

capsicum and caper mayonnaise

¼ cup (75g) mayonnaise

⅓ cup (65g) char-grilled red capsicum (bell peppers), chopped finely

1 tablespoon rinsed, drained capers, chopped coarsely

1 Using a meat mallet, gently pound chicken between pieces of plastic wrap until 1cm (½-inch) thick. Toss chicken in flour; shake away excess. Dip into combined egg and milk then breadcrumbs. Cover; refrigerate for 1 hour.
2 Meanwhile, make capsicum and caper mayonnaise.
3 Heat 1 tablespoon of the oil in a large frying pan over low heat; cook onion, stirring occasionally, for 15 minutes or until caramelised. Transfer to a small bowl; cover to keep warm.
4 Heat remaining oil in same cleaned pan over medium heat; cook chicken, in batches, until cooked through. Drain on absorbent paper towel; cover to keep warm.
5 Meanwhile, split bread pieces in half; toast cut sides. Sandwich chicken, onion, mayonnaise and lettuce between toast halves.
**capsicum and caper mayonnaise** Combine ingredients in a small bowl. Cover; refrigerate until required.

**prep + cook time** 1½ hours (+ refrigeration) **serves** 4
**tip** For toddlers, cut part of one of the schnitzels into finger-sized pieces and serve with tomato sauce instead of the capsicum and caper mayonnaise. You can use your favourite type of bread instead of the turkish bread.

There are many different varieties of lavash breads available from supermarkets; choose your favourite for this recipe.

# tuna and carrot pinwheels

185g (6 ounces) canned tuna in springwater, drained

1 small carrot (70g), grated finely

¼ cup (75g) mayonnaise

6 slices lavash or mountain bread

2 tablespoons mayonnaise, extra

**1** Combine tuna, carrot and mayonnaise in a medium bowl.

**2** Spread one slice of bread with one third of the extra mayonnaise; top with another piece of bread. Spread one third of the tuna mixture along one short edge of the bread. Roll bread tightly; trim edges. Using a serrated knife, cut roll into four pieces. Repeat with remaining bread, extra mayonnaise and tuna mixture.

**prep time** 20 minutes **makes** 12

# chicken, avocado and cream cheese sandwich

¼ cup (40g) coarsely chopped cooked chicken

¼ small avocado (50g), chopped coarsely

1 teaspoon lemon juice

1 tablespoon spreadable cream cheese

2 slices multi-grain bread (90g)

¼ cup loosely packed mixed salad leaves

**1** Combine chicken, avocado and juice in a small bowl.
**2** Spread cream cheese on one slice of bread; top with chicken mixture, salad leaves and another slice of bread. Cut sandwich into squares or triangles.

**prep time** 10 minutes **serves** 1

**tip** We used barbecue chicken in this recipe; you could use left-over roast chicken or any cooked chicken you have on hand.

# corned beef and pickle rolls

4 small white or wholemeal dinner rolls (120g), cut in half

2 tablespoons sweet mustard pickle

2 slices corned beef (60g), halved

2 slices cheddar (50g), halved

**1** Spread rolls with pickle. Sandwich corned beef and cheese between rolls.

**prep time** 5 minutes **makes** 4

**tip** This traditional recipe is a great standby. You can use leftover corned beef from the night before or you can buy it ready-sliced from the supermarket deli section.

chicken, avocado and cream cheese sandwich

corned beef and pickle rolls

You can substitute kumara for the pumpkin. Use lebanese bread as the pizza base if you wish. We used a passata sauce, which is just a plain tomato pasta sauce – it is available at the supermarket.

## pumpkin and fetta pizza

200g (6½-ounce) piece pumpkin, peeled

2 x 220g (7-ounce) pizza bases

⅔ cup (170g) bottled tomato pasta sauce

100g (3 ounces) fetta, crumbled

1 Preheat oven to 180°C/350°F. Oil two oven trays or pizza pans.

2 Using a vegetable peeler, slice pumpkin into thin strips.

3 Place pizza bases on trays; spread with sauce, then top with pumpkin. Spray with cooking-oil spray; sprinkle with cheese.

4 Bake pizzas for 10 minutes or until pumpkin is tender and pizza bases are crisp.

**prep + cook time** 25 minutes  **serves** 4

# corn, zucchini and egg sandwich

2 tablespoons canned corn kernels

½ small zucchini (45g), grated coarsely

2 teaspoons mayonnaise

1 hard-boiled egg, mashed

2 slices white sandwich bread (90g)

1 Combine corn, zucchini, mayonnaise and egg in a small bowl.
2 Sandwich egg mixture between bread slices. Cut into squares or triangles.

**prep time** 10 minutes **serves** 1

**tip** Swap the white bread for a wholemeal or multi-grain bread.

# chicken, celery and avocado sandwich

⅓ cup (50g) finely shredded cooked chicken

1 trimmed celery stick (100g), chopped finely

¼ small avocado (50g), mashed

1 teaspoon lemon juice

2 slices white sandwich bread (90g)

1 Combine chicken, celery, avocado and juice in a small bowl.
2 Sandwich chicken mixture between bread slices. Cut into squares or triangles.

**prep time** 10 minutes **serves** 1

**tips** We used barbecue chicken in this recipe; you could use left-over roast chicken or any cooked chicken you have on hand. Swap the white bread for wholemeal or multi-grain.

corn, zucchini and egg sandwich

chicken, celery and avocado sandwich

# bean and coriander quesadillas

840g (1¾ pounds) canned mexe-beans, drained

16 mini (15cm/6-inch) flour tortillas (400g)

2 large tomatoes (440g), seeds removed, chopped finely

½ cup coarsely chopped fresh coriander (cilantro)

1½ cups (180g) coarsely grated cheddar

1 Preheat a sandwich press.

2 Mash beans with a fork. Spread beans over eight tortillas; sprinkle with tomato, coriander and cheese. Top with the other eight tortillas.

3 Cook quesadillas in the sandwich press until browned and heated through; cut into wedges. Adults can drizzle quesadillas with a squeeze of lime or lemon.

**prep + cook time** 20 minutes **serves** 4

**tips**  If you don't have a sandwich press, cook the quesadillas under a preheated grill (broiler), turning once, until they are browned both sides and crisp.

**serving suggestion**  Sour cream and sliced avocado.

# DINNER

Instil good eating habits by having the family all sitting around the dining room table at dinner time; focus on the meal, without the distraction of the television and/or smart phones, tablets, or computer games.

## beef, tomato and pea pies

*You need a 12cm (5-inch) and a 9cm (3½-inch) round cutter.*

1 tablespoon vegetable oil

1 small brown onion (80g), chopped finely

300g (9½ ounces) minced (ground) beef

400g (12½ ounces) canned crushed tomatoes

1 tablespoon tomato paste

2 tablespoons worcestershire sauce

½ cup (125ml) beef stock

½ cup (60g) frozen peas

3 sheets puff pastry

1 egg, beaten lightly

**1** Heat oil in a large saucepan over medium heat; cook onion, stirring, for 4 minutes or until soft. Add the beef; cook, stirring, for 5 minutes or until brown. Add tomatoes, paste, sauce and stock; bring to the boil. Reduce heat; simmer, uncovered, for 20 minutes or until sauce is thick. Stir in peas.

**2** Oil a 6-hole (¾-cup/180ml) texas muffin pan. Cut 6 x 12cm (5-inch) rounds and 6 x 9cm (3½-inch) rounds from pastry. Ease large pastry rounds into pan holes, press into base and sides; trim edges. Refrigerate for 30 minutes.

**3** Preheat oven to 220°C/425°F.

**4** Line pastry with baking paper; fill with dried beans or rice. Bake for 10 minutes; remove paper and beans, cool.

**5** Fill pastry cases with beef mixture; brush edges with egg. Top with remaining pastry rounds; press edges to seal. Brush tops with egg.

**6** Bake for 20 minutes or until mixture is heated and pastry is golden. Stand pies for 5 minutes before removing from pan.

**prep + cook time** 1¼ hours (+ refrigeration) **makes** 6

**tips** Cooked pies can be frozen for up to 3 months; store between layers of baking paper in an airtight container in the freezer. Thaw overnight in the fridge before reheating in a 180°C/350°F oven for about 25 minutes or until hot.

**serving suggestion** Tomato sauce, creamy mashed potato, steamed vegetables or a salad.

# sesame chicken stir-fry

345g (11 ounces) bean thread noodles

1 tablespoon sesame seeds

1 tablespoon peanut oil

2 chicken breast fillets (400g), sliced thinly

1 medium brown onion (150g), peeled, sliced thinly

1 clove garlic, crushed

280g (9 ounces) broccolini, chopped coarsely

2 tablespoons fish sauce

1 tablespoon sweet chilli sauce

2 tablespoons dark soy sauce

4 green onions (scallions), sliced thinly

1 cup (80g) bean sprouts

**1** Place noodles in a medium heatproof bowl; cover with boiling water. Stand for 5 minutes or until tender; drain.
**2** Heat wok over medium heat; cook sesame seeds, stirring, for 1 minute or until browned lightly. Remove from wok.
**3** Heat half the oil in wok over high heat. Stir-fry chicken, in batches, until browned all over; remove from wok.
**4** Heat remaining oil in wok; stir-fry brown onion, garlic and broccolini, over high heat, for 3 minutes or until onion is soft.
**5** Return chicken to wok with noodles, sesame seeds, sauces, half the green onion and half the sprouts; stir-fry 2 minutes or until heated through.
**6** To serve, top stir-fry with remaining green onion and bean sprouts.

**prep + cook time** 40 minutes  **serves** 4
**tip** Cut noodles into bite-sized pieces for toddlers. You can use kitchen scissors to cut the green onions into thin slices – this is a quick and easy way to do it.

# salmon pasta

375g (12 ounces) angel hair pasta

4 cloves garlic, crushed

250g (8 ounces) cherry tomatoes, halved

400g (12½ ounces) canned salmon, drained

**1** Cook pasta in a large saucepan of boiling water until tender; drain, reserving ¼ cup of the cooking liquid. Rinse pasta under cold water, drain.

**2** Meanwhile, cook garlic and tomato in a heated oiled medium frying pan over medium-high heat, stirring, for 5 minutes or until tomato softens.

**3** Return pasta to pan with reserved liquid, tomato and salmon; toss until heated through.

**prep + cook time** 20 minutes  **serves** 4
**tips**  You can swap the salmon for tuna or chicken, if you like. Chop pasta into bite-sized pieces for toddlers.

# bbq pork spare ribs

1 cup (250ml) tomato sauce

¼ cup (60ml) worcestershire sauce

½ cup (110g) firmly packed brown sugar

2kg (4 pounds) slabs american-style pork spareribs

1 Combine sauces and sugar in a medium saucepan; bring to the boil. Remove from heat; cool marinade for 10 minutes.
2 Place pork in a large shallow baking dish, pour marinade all over pork; cover, refrigerate for 3 hours or overnight, turning pork occasionally.

3 Drain pork; reserve marinade. Cook pork on a heated oiled grill plate (or grill or barbecue) for 30 minutes or until cooked through, turning and brushing frequently with some of the reserved marinade.
4 Boil remaining marinade in a small saucepan for 5 minutes or until thickened slightly.
5 Cut spareribs into portions; serve with marinade.

**prep + cook time** 45 minutes (+ refrigeration) **serves** 4
**serving suggestion** Serve these with char-grilled potatoes and a leafy green salad. Baby new potatoes, also known as chats, are perfect. You can steam or boil chat potatoes whole without peeling them. Dry them before grilling.

# moroccan spiced fish

1 tablespoon moroccan seasoning

2 tablespoons lime juice

1 tablespoon vegetable oil

4 x 200g (6½ ounces) firm white fish fillets

**1** Combine seasoning, juice and oil in a large bowl; add fish, turn to coat in mixture.
**2** Cook fish on a heated oiled grill plate (or grill or barbecue) until fish is just cooked.

**prep + cook time** 20 minutes  **serves** 4

**tip**  You can use any of your favourite white fish fillets for this recipe like bream, flathead, whiting, snapper, redfish, dhufish, and ling.

**serving suggestion**  Accompany with lime wedges, and slices of tomato and cucumber, and a green leafy salad.

# lamb rack with tomatoes

4 x 4 french-trimmed lamb cutlet racks (720g)

olive oil cooking spray

2 teaspoons mixed dried herbs

500g (1 pound) cherry truss tomatoes

2 tablespoons balsamic vinegar

**1** Preheat oven to 200°C/400°F.
**2** Spray lamb with oil; sprinkle with herbs. Place lamb in a large oiled baking dish.
**3** Roast lamb, uncovered, for 15 minutes. Place tomatoes around lamb, drizzle with vinegar. Roast lamb for a further 10 minutes or until it is cooked as desired and tomatoes have started to soften. Cover; stand for 10 minutes before slicing.

**prep + cook time** 50 minutes  **serves** 4

**tip**  Roasting cherry tomatoes intensifies their flavour and transforms them into a lovely accompaniment to the lamb. Cut lamb into bite-sized pieces for younger toddlers.

**serving suggestion**  Roasted baby carrots.

moroccan spiced fish

lamb rack with tomatoes

# beef enchiladas

2 tablespoons olive oil

1 small yellow capsicum (bell pepper) (150g), chopped finely

1 small red onion (100g), chopped finely

1 clove garlic, crushed

1 teaspoon ground cumin

½ teaspoon sweet paprika

400g (12½ ounces) ground (minced) beef

2 tablespoons tomato paste

2 tablespoons water

130g (4 ounces) canned kidney beans, rinsed, drained

1 tablespoon coarsely chopped fresh oregano

2 cups (500ml) bottled tomato pasta sauce

1 cup (250ml) water, extra

10 x 15cm (6-inch) corn or flour tortillas

1 cup (120g) coarsely grated cheddar

1 tablespoon finely chopped fresh flat-leaf parsley

**1** Heat half the oil in a large frying pan over high heat; cook capsicum, half the onion and half the garlic, stirring, for about 3 minutes or until vegetables soften. Add spices; cook, stirring, until fragrant. Add mince; cook, stirring, for 5 minutes or until changed in colour. Stir in paste and the 2 tablespoons of water; simmer, stirring, for 1 minute. Place filling mixture into a large heatproof bowl; stir in beans and oregano.

**2** Heat remaining oil in same cleaned pan over high heat; cook remaining onion and garlic, stirring, for 3 minutes or until onion softens. Add pasta sauce and the extra water to pan; bring to the boil. Reduce heat; simmer, uncovered, for 5 minutes.

**3** Preheat oven to 180°C/350°F. Oil a shallow square 3-litre (12-cup) ovenproof dish. Spread ½ cup pasta sauce mixture evenly over base of dish.

**4** Warm tortillas according to package instructions. Dip one side of tortillas, one at a time, in pasta sauce mixture; place, sauce-side up, on a board. Divide filling among tortillas, placing mixture on edge of tortilla; roll tortillas to enclose filling.

**5** Place enchiladas, seam-side down, snugly in a single layer, in dish. Spread remaining pasta sauce mixture over enchiladas; sprinkle with cheese. Cook, uncovered, for 15 minutes or until enchiladas are hot.

**6** Serve enchiladas sprinkled with parsley and, if you like, sour cream, shredded lettuce and chopped fresh tomatoes.

**prep + cook time** 1¼ hours  **serves** 4

**tip**  Cut your toddler's serving into bite-sized pieces. The beef mixture can be made a day ahead; store, covered, in the fridge.

# baked chicken with rosemary and potatoes

750g (1½ pounds) unpeeled medium potatoes, quartered

2 tablespoons coarsely chopped fresh rosemary leaves

1 lemon (140g)

8 chicken drumsticks (1.2kg)

**1** Preheat oven to 200°C/400°F. Oil a large shallow baking dish.
**2** Combine potato and rosemary in dish. Remove strips of rind from lemon using a vegetable peeler; squeeze juice from lemon over potatoes. Roast, uncovered, for 20 minutes.
**3** Meanwhile, cook chicken in a heated oiled large frying pan over medium heat, about 5 minutes or until browned all over.
**4** Remove dish from oven; place chicken on top of potato; add rind. Cover dish with foil; roast 20 minutes. Uncover; roast for 30 minutes or until chicken is cooked and potato is tender.

**prep + cook time** 1½ hours  **serves** 4
**tip** This is an easy dish that you can leave to roast in the oven while getting everyone ready for dinner. Children love being able to pick up chicken drumsticks in their hands and not having to bother with knives and forks.
**serving suggestion** Steamed green beans.

# ocean trout fillet with creamy chive sauce

4 x 220g (7 ounces) ocean trout fillets, skin on

300ml pouring cream

¼ cup (60ml) lemon juice

1 tablespoon finely chopped fresh chives

**1** Cook fish, skin-side down, on a heated oiled grill plate (or grill or barbecue), over high heat, for 5 minutes. Turn fish; cook for 3 minutes or until just cooked (the fish should still be pink in the centre). Remove fish from pan; cover to keep warm.
**2** Meanwhile, combine cream and juice in a small saucepan; simmer, uncovered, for 5 minutes or until sauce thickens slightly. Stir in chives.
**3** Serve fish drizzled with sauce.

**prep + cook time** 25 minutes  **serves** 4
**tips** Fish should be an important part of everyone's diet. Ocean trout is high in omega-3, essential for a healthy heart; it has a great flavour and texture, is available all year, and can be used in a wide range of dishes. It is the perfect fish to include in your midweek meals.
**serving suggestion** Steamed baby peas.

baked chicken with rosemary and potatoes

ocean trout fillet with creamy chive sauce

# Snacks

## frozen yoghurt and raspberry swirl

Combine ⅔ cup (150g) caster (superfine) sugar and ⅓ cup (80ml) water in a small saucepan; stir over low heat until sugar dissolves. Sprinkle 1 teaspoon gelatine over sugar syrup mixture; stir until gelatine dissolves. Combine gelatine mixture and 500g (1 pound) greek-style yoghurt in a medium bowl; pour into a 14cm x 21cm (5½-inch x 8½-inch) loaf pan. Cover; freeze for 4 hours or until almost firm. Push 120g (4 ounces) thawed frozen raspberries through a fine sieve over a small bowl; discard seeds. Scrape yoghurt from bottom and sides of pan with a fork; swirl raspberry purée through yoghurt. Cover; freeze until ready to serve. Serve with fresh raspberries, if you like.

**prep + cook time** 20 minutes (+ freezing) **serves** 4
**tip** Break up a few tablespoons of the frozen yoghurt and raspberry swirl with a fork for your toddler.

## mini chocolate muffins

Preheat oven to 180°C/350°F. Line two 12-hole mini muffin pans (1-tablespoon/20ml) with paper cases. Combine ¾ cup (110g) self-raising flour, ⅓ cup (75g) firmly packed brown sugar and ¼ cup (20g) rolled oats in a medium bowl. Combine 1 egg, ¼ cup milk, ¼ cup apple juice and ¼ cup vegetable oil; stir into the flour mixture. Add half a finely chopped medium ripe banana (100g) and 50g (1½ ounces) finely grated dark chocolate; stir gently to just combine. Divide mixture into pan holes. Bake for 15 minutes or until a skewer inserted into the middle comes out clean. Stand muffins in pans for 5 minutes before turning, top-side up, onto wire racks; sprinkle warm cakes with an extra 50g (1½ ounces) finely grated dark chocolate. Cool muffins.

**prep + cook time** 30 minutes **makes** 24
**tip** Muffins can be stored in an airtight container for 3 days, or frozen for up to 3 months.

# hummus

Rinse and drain 2 x 300g (9½-ounce) cans chickpeas. Cook chickpeas in a medium saucepan of boiling water, uncovered, for 15 minutes or until tender; drain. Cool 10 minutes. Blend or process chickpeas with 2 tablespoons olive oil, 2 teaspoons lemon juice, 1 crushed garlic clove and 1 cup plain yoghurt until smooth.

**prep + cook time** 25 minutes (+ cooling) **makes** 2 cups
**tips** Store hummus, covered, in the fridge for up to 3 days. Serve hummus with pitta bread triangles or sticks of blanched carrots and cucumbers, or snow peas.

# fruit skewers with caramel yoghurt

Peel and core ½ medium pineapple (625g); cut pineapple into 2.5cm (1-inch) lengths then crossways into 3cm (1¼-inch) pieces. Segment 2 large oranges (600g). Hull 250g (8 ounces) strawberries; cut in half crossways. Cut 2 large bananas (460g), into 3cm (1¼-inch) slices. Thread pineapple alternately with orange segments, strawberry halves and banana slices onto 12 x 20cm (8-inch) bamboo skewers; place on an oven tray. Stir 30g (1 ounce) butter, ¼ cup (55g) firmly packed brown sugar and 1 tablespoon lemon juice in a small saucepan over low heat until butter melts and sugar dissolves. Pour mixture over skewers, coating all fruit pieces. Cook, in batches, on a heated greased grill plate (or grill or barbecue) for 5 minutes or until browned. Serve skewers with 1 cup (280g) honey yoghurt.

**prep + cook time** 40 minutes **serves** 4
**tips** You can swap the fruit for your child's favourite. If you don't want to cook the fruit, omit the caramel mixture, and serve the plain fruit skewers with yoghurt.

veal with creamy thyme sauce

brown rice pilaf

# veal with creamy thyme sauce

500g (1 pound) veal schnitzels

300ml pouring cream

1 tablespoon dijon mustard

1 tablespoon fresh thyme leaves

**1** Cook veal in a heated oiled large frying pan, in batches, over high heat, for 1 minute each side or until browned. Cover to keep warm.
**2** Add cream, mustard and thyme to pan; bring to the boil, stirring. Simmer, uncovered, about 5 minutes or until sauce thickens slightly.
**3** Top veal with sauce to serve.

**prep + cook time** 20 minutes  **serves** 4
**tip**  Veal schnitzel is thinly sliced steak available crumbed or plain (uncrumbed); we use plain uncrumbed schnitzel, sometimes called escalopes, in our recipe. Because veal schnitzels are a very lean cut of meat, they dry out quickly if overcooked. Fry them over a high heat for a short time.
**serving suggestion** Steamed baby new potatoes and broccoli and mashed pumpkin.

# brown rice pilaf

*This recipe is gluten-, wheat-, dairy-, egg-, and nut-free.*

1 medium kumara (orange sweet potato) (200g), chopped coarsely

cooking-oil spray

1 medium lemon (140g)

1 cup (250ml) salt-reduced gluten-free vegetable stock

2 cups (500ml) water

2 teaspoons olive oil

1 medium brown onion (150g), chopped finely

2 trimmed celery sticks (200g), sliced thinly

2 cloves garlic, crushed

150g (4½ ounces) button mushrooms, halved

1½ cups (300g) brown medium-grain rice

¾ cup loosely packed fresh flat-leaf parsley leaves, chopped coarsely

**1** Preheat oven to 180°C/350°F.
**2** Place kumara on a baking-paper-lined oven tray; spray lightly with oil. Roast for 25 minutes or until tender.
**3** Use a vegetable peeler to remove 2 strips of rind from the lemon.
**4** Meanwhile, place stock and the water in a small saucepan; bring to the boil. Reduce heat; simmer, covered.
**5** Heat oil in a medium saucepan over high heat; cook onion, celery and garlic, stirring, for 3 minutes or until onion softens. Add mushrooms and rice to pan; cook, stirring, for 2 minutes. Add hot stock mixture, reduce heat; simmer, covered, for 40 minutes or until stock is absorbed and rice is tender. Stir in kumara, rind and parsley.

**prep + cook time** 1¼ hours  **serves** 4
**tip**  You can swap the kumara for pumpkin. If your child likes a little more flavour, swap the parsley for coriander (cilantro).

# PARTY FOOD

At this age, kids are still more interested in the party games than the variety of food on offer. If possible, get them outside expending energy with a treasure or jewellery hunt. Or theme the party according to your child's favourite hobby, book or colour.

## chocolate on chocolate cakes

*This recipe is gluten-free.*

200g (6½ ounces) butter, softened

2¼ cups (300g) gluten-free self-raising flour

¼ cup (25g) cocoa powder

1 cup (220g) caster (superfine) sugar

¾ cup (180ml) milk

2 eggs

2 egg whites

chocolate icing

1 cup (160g) pure icing (confectioners') sugar

1 tablespoon cocoa powder

2 tablespoons water

**1** Preheat oven to 180°C/350°F. Line two 12-hole (⅓-cup/80ml) muffin pans with paper cases.
**2** Beat butter in a large bowl with an electric mixer until pale. Beat sifted flour, cocoa and ¼ cup of the sugar alternately with milk into butter, in two batches, until combined.
**3** Beat eggs and egg whites in a small bowl with an electric mixer until thick and creamy. Gradually add remaining sugar, one tablespoon at a time, beating until sugar dissolves between additions. Gradually beat egg mixture into flour mixture until combined.
**4** Drop 2½ tablespoons of mixture into each paper case; bake cakes about 20 minutes. Turn, top-side-up, onto wire racks to cool.
**5** Make chocolate icing. Spread cold cakes with icing.
**chocolate icing** Sift sugar and sifted cocoa into a small bowl; stir in the water.

**prep + cook time** 40 minutes (+ cooling) **makes** 24
**tips** Store cakes in an airtight container for up to 2 days. Un-iced cakes can be frozen for up to 2 months. For a dairy-free version of this cake, substitute dairy-free spread for the butter and soy milk for the milk; the rest of the recipe stays the same. You can substitute ordinary self-raising flour for the gluten-free flour if no one has a gluten allergy.

# pizza fingers

430g (14-ounce) loaf turkish bread, cut into
2cm (1-inch) slices

¼ cup (65g) basil pesto

⅓ cup (50g) semi-dried tomatoes in oil, drained,
chopped finely

10 cherry bocconcini cheese (150g), sliced thinly

¼ cup (70g) tomato paste

⅓ cup (90g) drained canned pineapple pieces,
chopped coarsely

2 rindless bacon slices (130g), sliced thinly

½ cup (60g) coarsely grated cheddar

2 tablespoons small fresh basil leaves

1 Preheat oven to 180°C/350°F. Line two oven trays with baking paper.
2 Place bread, cut-side up, onto oven trays. Bake for 10 minutes or until the bread is crisp.
3 Spread half the bread slices with pesto; top with semi-dried tomato and bocconcini. Spread the remaining bread slices with tomato paste; top with pineapple, bacon and cheddar.
4 Bake for 12 minutes or until cheese melts. Sprinkle with basil to serve.

**prep + cook time** 30 minutes  **makes** 20

**tip** These pizzas can be prepared 2 hours ahead to the end of step 3. Cover and refrigerate until you are ready to bake.

# rainbow meringues

*You need 3 piping bags (one for each colour) fitted with a 5mm (¼-inch) fluted tube, so it's probably best to use disposable bags (available from larger supermarkets). Wash and dry the tube after piping each colour.*

2 egg whites

½ cup (110g) caster (superfine) sugar

pink, yellow and green food colouring

¼ cup (50g) mixed glacé cherries, chopped coarsely

1 Preheat oven to 120°C/250°F. Grease and line two oven trays.
2 Beat egg whites in a small bowl with an electric mixer until soft peaks form. Gradually add sugar, beating until dissolved between additions.
3 Divide mixture into 3 separate bowls; tint each with one of the food colourings.
4 Spoon mixture into the piping bag; pipe meringues onto trays 2cm (¾-inch) apart; top each with a piece of cherry.
5 Bake meringues for 45 minutes; cool in oven with door ajar.

**prep + cook time** 55 minutes  (+ cooling)  **makes** 30
**tip**  Meringues can be made a day ahead; store them in an airtight container.

# sticky apricot chicken wings

8 large chicken wings (800g)

⅓ cup (110g) apricot jam

1 teaspoon sweet paprika

2 tablespoons lemon juice

1 Preheat oven to 200°C/400°F.
2 Combine wings, jam, paprika and juice in a large bowl.
3 Place undrained wings, in a single layer, in a large baking dish. Roast, uncovered, for 35 minutes or until wings are cooked through. Cool.

**prep + cook time** 45 minutes (+ cooling)  **makes** 8
**tips**  The wings can be prepared the day before, keep them covered in the fridge. Serve with lemon wedges, if you like.

rainbow meringues

sticky apricot chicken wings

# mandarin and poppy seed friands

2 large mandarins (500g), unpeeled

1 tablespoon poppy seeds

2 tablespoons mandarin juice

6 egg whites

1½ cups (240g) icing (confectioners') sugar

½ cup (75g) plain (all-purpose) flour

185g (6 ounces) butter, melted

1 cup (120g) ground almonds

**1** Preheat oven to 200°C/400°F. Grease a 12-hole (½-cup/125ml) oval friand pan.

**2** Finely grate rind from mandarins (you need 1 tablespoon of rind). Juice mandarins (you need 2 tablespoons of juice).

**3** Combine poppy seeds and juice in a small jug; stand for 10 minutes.

**4** Lightly whisk egg whites in a medium bowl with a fork. Sift icing sugar and flour into the bowl. Add butter, ground almonds, rind and poppy seed mixture; stir until combined. Spoon mixture into pan holes.

**5** Bake about 15 minutes. Stand friands in pan for 5 minutes before turning, top-side up, onto wire racks to cool.

**prep + cook time** 40 minutes  **makes** 12

**tips** Store friands, in an airtight container, for up to 3 days. Serve dusted with sifted icing (confectioners') sugar, if you like. To transform these into lemon and poppy seed friands, simply use lemon rind instead of mandarin rind and lemon juice instead of mandarin juice.

# chicken and avocado rice paper rolls

12 x 17cm (6¾-inch) square rice paper sheets

½ medium avocado (125g), sliced thinly

1¼ cups (200g) finely shredded barbecued chicken

50g (1½ ounces) snow pea sprouts, trimmed

**1** Place one sheet of rice paper in a medium bowl of warm water until just softened; lift sheet carefully from water, place on a board covered with a clean tea towel with a corner point facing towards you. Place one slice of avocado vertically down the centre of the rice paper, then top with chicken and sprouts.
**2** Fold top and bottom corner points over filling; roll rice paper sheet over to enclose filling. Repeat with remaining rice paper sheets and ingredients. Serve with soy or sweet chilli sauce for dipping, if you like.

**prep time** 25 minutes  **makes** 12
**tips**  Rice paper rolls can be made a day ahead. To stop rice paper rolls from drying out, wrap them in a moist absorbent towel, then in plastic wrap; store in the fridge.

**tip** You can substitute potato or pumpkin for the kumara, or use a combination of all three – it will be just as delicious. Triangles can be made a day ahead to the end of step 3; cover, and refrigerate until ready to bake.

# kumara, corn and spinach triangles

1 medium kumara (orange sweet potato) (400g), chopped finely

250g (8 ounces) frozen spinach, thawed, drained

620g (1¼ pounds) canned creamed corn

4 sheets ready-rolled shortcrust pastry

**1** Preheat oven to 200°C/400°F. Grease and line two oven trays.
**2** Cook kumara in a heated oiled large frying pan over high heat, stirring, until browned lightly and tender. Combine kumara, spinach and corn in a large bowl.
**3** Cut pastry sheets into quarters. Place equal amounts of filling near the centre of each square. Lightly moisten pastry edges with a little water; fold pastry in half to form a triangle. Press edges together with a fork to seal.
**4** Place triangles on trays; spray with oil. Bake triangles for 15 minutes or until browned lightly.

**prep + cook time** 45 minutes  **makes** 16

# seeing stripes at four

*You need a 23cm x 34cm (9¼-inch x 13½-inch) number 4 cake pan, and a 25cm x 40cm (10-inch x 16-inch) rectangular cake board.*

3 x 340g (11-ounce) packets butter cake mix

7 pink fruit sticks

6 orange fruit sticks

6 green fruit sticks

6 yellow fruit sticks

butter cream

125g (4 ounces) butter

1½ cups (160g) icing (confectioners') sugar

1 tablespoon milk

blue food colouring

1 Preheat oven to 180°C/350°F. Grease the number 4 cake pan; line base with baking paper.

2 Make cakes according to directions on packets; pour mixture into pan. Bake for about 50 minutes. Stand cake in pan for 5 minutes before turning, top-side up, onto a wire rack to cool.

3 Meanwhile, make butter cream.

4 Using a serrated knife, level cake top; secure cake to the cake board with a little butter cream.

5 Spread butter cream all over cake.

6 Using a sharp pair of scissors, trim each fruit stick to fit across the cake. Using the picture as a guide, decorate cake with fruit sticks.

**butter frosting** Beat butter in a small bowl with an electric mixer until as white as possible. Gradually beat in half the sifted icing sugar, milk then remaining icing sugar. Tint butter cream blue.

**prep + cook time** 2 hours (+ cooling) **serves** 18

**tips** Use a gluten-free packet cake mix for this recipe, if you like. Just make sure the ingredients for the butter cream and the decorations are also gluten-free. Cake can be made and decorated a day ahead. Store in a cool, dry place. Number 4 cake pans can be hired from cake decorating suppliers.

# a superstar at five

*You need eight 10cm (4-inch) lengths of florists' wire, small and large star-shaped cutters, a 20cm x 34cm (8-inch x 13½-inch) number 5 cake pan and a 25cm x 40cm (10-inch x 16-inch) rectangular cake board. You need to make the decorations the day before.*

200g (6½ ounces) ready-made white icing

----

pure icing (confectioners') sugar, for dusting

----

blue food colouring

----

2 x 340g (11-ounce) packets butter cake mix

----

butter cream

----

185g (6 ounces) butter

----

2¼ cups (280g) icing (confectioners') sugar

----

1½ tablespoons milk

----

yellow food colouring

----

**1** Knead ready-made icing on a surface dusted with a little sifted icing sugar until icing loses its stickiness; divide icing in half. Tint one portion blue; tint the other portion a darker blue. Roll out each colour, one at a time, until 5mm (¼-inch) thick. Using a 3cm (1¼-inch) five-pointed star cutter and a 5cm (2-inch) six-pointed star cutter, cut out star shapes from both icings.

**2** Using the picture as a guide; bend the florists' wire. Wet one end of each length of wire; push the damp ends into some of the smaller stars. Place stars on a baking-paper-lined tray; stand overnight to dry.

**3** Preheat oven to 180°C/350°F. Grease the number 5 cake pan; line base with baking paper.

**4** Make cakes according to directions on packets; pour mixture into pan. Bake about 45 minutes. Stand cake in the pan for 5 minutes before turning, top-side up, onto a wire rack to cool.

**5** Meanwhile, make butter cream. Using a serrated knife, level cake top; secure cake to cake board with a little butter cream.

**6** Spread butter cream all over cake.

**7** Using the picture as a guide, position stars on cake.

**butter frosting** Beat butter in a small bowl with an electric mixer until as white as possible. Gradually beat in half the sifted icing sugar, milk then remaining icing sugar. Tint the butter cream yellow.

**prep + cook time** 2½ hours (+ standing & cooling) **serves** 18
**tips** Use gluten-free packet cake mix for this recipe, if you like. Just make sure the ingredients for the butter cream and the decorations are also gluten-free. Cake can be made and decorated a day ahead. Number 5 cake pans can be hired from cake decorating suppliers.

# glossary

**arrowroot** a starch made from a Central American plant; used mostly as a thickener. The lack of gluten in arrowroot makes it ideal as a replacement for wheat flour in baking. Arrowroot is used to thicken sauces and create glazes that require a clear glossy appearance.

**bacon slices** also known as rashers of bacon; made from cured and smoked pork side.

**baking paper** also known as parchment, silicon paper or non-stick baking paper; not to be confused with greaseproof or waxed paper. Used for lining baking pans and oven trays so cakes and biscuits won't stick, making removal easy.

**baking powder** a raising agent consisting mainly of two parts cream of tartar to one part bicarbonate of soda (baking soda).

*gluten-free* a raising agent suitable for people with an allergic response to glutens or seeking an alternative to everyday baking powder.

**beans**

*borlotti* also known as roman beans or pink beans; available fresh or dried. Interchangeable with pinto beans because both are pale pink or beige with dark red streaks.

*kidney* medium-sized red bean, slightly floury in texture yet sweet in flavour; sold dried or canned.

*mexe (mexican-style)* are a mildly spiced canned combination of kidney or pinto beans, capsicum and tomato.

*white* a generic term we use for canned or dried cannellini, haricot, navy or great northern beans, all of which can be substituted for the other.

**bean thread noodles** also known as wun sen, made from extruded mung bean paste; also known as cellophane or glass noodles because they are transparent when cooked. White in colour (not off-white like rice vermicelli), very delicate and fine; available dried in various-sized bundles. Must be soaked to soften before use.

**bicarbonate of soda** also known as baking soda.

**breadcrumbs, packaged** fine-textured, crunchy, white breadcrumbs.

**broccolini** a cross between broccoli and chinese kale; milder and sweeter than broccoli. Each long stem is topped by a loose floret that resembles broccoli; from floret to stem, broccolini is completely edible.

**buk choy** also known as bok choy, pak choi, chinese white cabbage or chinese chard; has a fresh, mild mustard taste. Use both stems and leaves. Baby buk choy, also known as pak kat farang or shanghai bok choy, is much smaller and more tender than buk choy. Its mildly acrid, distinctively appealing taste has made it one of the most commonly used Asian greens.

**butter** this book uses salted butter unless stated otherwise; 125g is equal to 1 stick (4 ounces) butter.

**buttermilk** originally the term given to the slightly sour liquid left after butter was churned from cream, today it is made similarly to yoghurt. Despite its name, buttermilk is actually low in fat.

**cachous** also called dragées in some countries; minuscule (3mm to 5mm) metallic-looking-but-edible confectionery balls used in cake decorating; available in silver, gold or various colours.

**capsicum** also known as bell pepper, or simply, pepper. Comes in many colours: red, green, yellow, orange and purplish-black. Be sure to discard seeds and membranes before use.

**cheese**

*cheddar* the most widely eaten cheese in the world, cheddar is a semi-hard cow's-milk cheese. It ranges in colour from white to pale yellow, and has a slightly crumbly texture if properly matured.

*cream* commonly called Philly or Philadelphia; a soft cow's-milk cheese. Also available as spreadable light cream cheese, a light version of Philadelphia – a blend of cottage and cream cheeses.

*mozzarella* a soft, spun-curd cheese. It has a low melting point and wonderfully elastic texture when heated and is used to add texture rather than flavour.

*parmesan* also known as parmigiano, parmesan is a hard, grainy cow's-milk cheese. The curd is salted in brine for a month before being aged for up to two years in humid conditions.

*pizza* a blend of grated mozzarella, cheddar and parmesan cheeses.

*ricotta* a soft, sweet, moist, white cow's-milk cheese with a slightly grainy texture. The name roughly translates as 'cooked again' and refers to ricotta's manufacture from a whey that is itself a by-product of other cheese making.

**chickpeas** also called garbanzos, hummus or channa; an irregularly round, sandy-coloured legume.

**chocolate**

*Choc bits* also called chocolate chips or chocolate morsels; available in milk, white and dark chocolate. Made of cocoa liquor, cocoa butter, sugar and an emulsifier; these hold their shape in baking and are ideal for decorating.

*choc melts* small discs of compounded milk, white or dark chocolate; ideal for melting and moulding.

*dark eating* also called semi-sweet or luxury chocolate; made of a high percentage of cocoa liquor and cocoa butter, and a little added sugar. We use dark eating chocolate unless stated otherwise.

*white eating* contains no cocoa solids but derives its sweet flavour from cocoa butter. Very sensitive to heat, so watch carefully when melting.

**chocolate hazelnut spread** also known as nutella; made of cocoa powder, hazelnuts, sugar and milk.

**cinnamon** dried inner bark of the shoots of the cinnamon tree; available in stick (quill) or ground form.

**cloves** dried flower buds of a tropical tree; can be used whole or in ground form. Has a strong scent and taste so use sparingly.

**cocoa powder** also known as unsweetened cocoa; cocoa beans (cacao seeds) that have been fermented, roasted and ground into a powder.

**coconut**

*desiccated* concentrated, dried, unsweetened and finely shredded coconut flesh.

*flaked* dried flaked coconut flesh.

*milk* not the juice found inside the fruit, but the diluted liquid from the second pressing of the white flesh (meat) of a mature coconut. Available in cans and cartons at supermarkets.

*shredded* unsweetened thin strips of dried coconut flesh.

**cornflour** also known as cornstarch. Available made from corn or wheat (wheaten cornflour contains gluten; it gives a lighter texture in cakes). It may be used for baking or as a thickening agent in cooking.

**coriander** when fresh is also known as pak chee, cilantro or chinese parsley; bright-green-leafed herb with a pungent flavour. This herb almost always comes with its roots attached as both the stems and roots of coriander are used in Thai cooking.

**couscous** a fine, grain-like cereal product made from semolina; a dough of semolina flour and water is sieved then dehydrated to produce minuscule even-sized pellets of couscous; it is rehydrated by steaming, or with the addition of a warm liquid, and swells to three or four times its original size.

**cream** we use fresh pouring cream, also known as single or pure cream. It has no additives, and has a minimum fat content of 35 per cent.

*thickened* a whipping cream that contains a thickener. Has a minimum fat content of 35 per cent.

**cream of tartar** the acid ingredient in baking powder; added to confectionery mixtures to help prevent sugar from crystallising. Keeps frostings creamy and improves volume when beating egg whites.

**currants, dried** tiny, almost black raisins so-named from the grape type native to Corinth, Greece. These are not the same as fresh currants, which are the fruit of a plant in the gooseberry family.

**custard apples** are a heart-shaped fruit with a pale green skin and large bumps. They have a soft, sweet, creamy white flesh that contains large inedible black seeds. To eat, simply cut in half and scoop out the white flesh. Only buy custard apples with green skin; if the skin has turned a purplish-black colour, they are past their best.

**custard powder** an instant mixture used to make pouring custard; similar to North American instant pudding mixes.

**dates** are green when unripe and turn yellow, golden brown, black or mahogany red – depending on the variety – as they ripen. Available fresh or dried, pitted or unpitted. The skin is thin and papery and the flesh is extremely sweet. Choose plump, soft dates with a smooth, shiny skin.

**dhal** the Hindi word for legumes and pulses; they are a good source of protein. Sometimes lentils may also be known as dhal.

**eggplant** also known as aubergine. Ranging in size from tiny to very large, and in colour from pale-green to deep-purple, eggplant has an equally wide variety of flavours. *Baby eggplant,* also known as finger or japanese eggplant, are very small and slender.

**eggs** if recipes in this book call for raw or barely cooked eggs exercise caution if there is a salmonella problem in your area, particularly in food eaten by children, pregnant women, the elderly and infirm.

**fish fillets, firm white** blue eye, bream, flathead, swordfish, ling, whiting, jewfish, snapper or sea perch are all good choices. Check for any small pieces of bone in the fillets and use tweezers to remove them.

**flour**

*buckwheat* a herb in the same plant family as rhubarb; not a cereal so it is gluten-free. The seeds are ground into a fine flour-like consistency.

*plain* an all-purpose flour made from wheat.

*rice* very fine, almost powdery, gluten-free flour; made from ground white rice.

*self-raising* plain flour sifted with baking powder in the proportion of 1 cup flour to 2 teaspoons baking powder. Also called self-rising flour.

*soy* made from ground soya beans.

**gelatine** we use dried (powdered) gelatine; it's also available in sheet form known as leaf gelatine. Three teaspoons of dried gelatine (8g or one sachet) is roughly equivalent to four gelatine leaves.

**ginger**

*fresh* also called green or root ginger; the thick gnarled root of a tropical plant. Can be kept, peeled, covered with dry sherry, in a jar and refrigerated, or frozen in an airtight container.

*glacé* fresh ginger root preserved in sugar syrup; crystallised ginger (sweetened with cane sugar) can be substituted if rinsed with warm water and dried before using.

*ground* also called powdered ginger; used as a flavouring in baking but cannot be substituted for fresh ginger.

**glacé fruit** fruit such as pineapple, apricots, peaches and pears that are cooked in a heavy sugar syrup then dried.

**glucose syrup** also called liquid glucose, made from wheat starch; used in jam and confectionery making. Available at health-food stores and supermarkets.

**golden syrup** a by-product of refined sugarcane; pure maple syrup or honey can be substituted.

**gravy beef** also known as beef shin or shank, cut from the lower shin.

**jam** also known as preserve or conserve; most often made from fruit.

**jelly crystals** a powdered mixture of gelatine, sweetener and artificial fruit flavouring that's used to make a moulded, translucent, quivering dessert. Also known as jello.

**kumara** the Polynesian name of an orange-fleshed sweet potato often confused with yam.

**lebanese cucumber** short, slender and thin-skinned. Probably the most popular variety because of its tender, edible skin, tiny, yielding seeds and sweet, fresh and flavoursome taste.

**leek** a member of the onion family, resembles the green shallot but is much larger and more subtle and mild in flavour. Leeks need to be washed to remove grit from the inside layers. Trim the roots, leaving enough intact to hold the layers together. Cut in half lengthwise, but avoid cutting through the root.

**maple syrup** distilled from the sap of sugar maple trees. Maple-flavoured syrup is not an adequate substitute for the real thing.

**mince** also known as ground meat.

**mushrooms**

**button** these are small, cultivated white mushrooms with a delicate, subtle flavour.

**shiitake, fresh** also known as chinese black, forest or golden oak mushrooms; although cultivated, they have the earthiness and taste of wild mushrooms. Are large and meaty.

**oil**

*cooking spray* we use a cholesterol-free cooking spray made from canola oil.

*olive* made from ripened olives. 'Extra virgin' and 'virgin' are the first and second press, respectively, of the olives and are therefore considered the best; the 'extra light' or 'light' on other types refers to taste not fat levels.

*vegetable* sourced from plant rather than animal fats.

**onion**

*green* also known as scallion or, incorrectly, shallot. An immature onion picked before the bulb has formed; has a long, bright-green edible stalk.

*red* also known as spanish, red spanish or bermuda onion; a large, sweet-flavoured, purple-red onion.

*shallots* also called french shallots, golden shallots or eschalots; small, brown-skinned, elongated members of the onion family.

*spring* have small white bulbs and long, narrow, green-leafed tops.

**papaya** also known as pawpaw or papaw; large, pear-shaped red-orange tropical fruit.

**parsnip** a long, white root vegetable with feathery green leaves. It is related to the carrot, which it resembles, although it has a paler colour and a stronger flavour.

**patty-pan squash** also known as crookneck or custard marrow pumpkins; a round, slightly flat summer squash being yellow to pale-green in colour and having a scalloped edge. Harvested young, it has firm white flesh and a distinct flavour.

**pearl barley** barley that has had its outer husk (bran) removed, and been steamed and polished before being used in cooking, much the same as rice.

**pizza bases** pre-packaged for home-made pizzas. They come in a variety of sizes (snack or family) and thicknesses (thin and crispy or thick), and taste great with your favourite pizza toppings.

**polenta** also called cornmeal; a flour-like cereal made of dried corn (maize). Also the name of the dish made from it.

**quinoa** pronounced keen-wa, is the seed of a leafy plant similar to spinach. It has a delicate, slightly nutty taste and chewy texture. Its cooking qualities are similar to that of rice. You can buy it in most health-food stores and some delicatessens; it spoils easily, so keep it sealed in a glass jar under refrigeration. It should be rinsed well then drained, before using.

**raisins** dried sweet grapes (traditionally muscatel grapes).

**ready-made white icing** also called soft icing, prepared, ready-to-roll fondant. Available in the baking section at most supermarkets.

**rhubarb** a plant with long, green-red stalks; becomes sweet and edible when cooked.

**rice milk** usually made from filtered water and brown rice. It has less protein and calcium than cow's milk, but is high in carbohydrates and contains no cholesterol or lactose. Rice milk is not as thick as dairy or soy milks, and has a somewhat translucent consistency and a slightly sweet flavour.

**risoni** small rice-shape pasta; very similar to another small pasta, orzo.

**rockmelon** also known as cantaloupe and musk melon. Cut them into squares and freeze for an icy treat.

**rolled oats** flattened oat grain rolled into flakes and used for porridge. Instant oats are also available, but use traditional oats for baking.

**rolled rice** flattened rice grains rolled into flakes; similar to rolled oats.

**sauce**

*fish* also called nam pla or nuoc nam; made from pulverised salted fermented fish, most often anchovies. Has a pungent smell and strong taste, so use sparingly.

*soy* also known as sieu, is made from fermented soya beans. We use a mild Japanese variety in our recipes; possibly the best table soy and the one to choose if you only want one variety.

*soy, dark* deep brown, almost black in colour; rich, with a thicker consistency than other types. Pungent but not particularly salty, it is good for marinating.

*soy, light* fairly thin in consistency and, while paler than the others, the saltiest tasting; used in dishes in which the natural colour of the ingredients is to be maintained. Not to be confused with salt-reduced or low-sodium soy sauces.

*oyster* Asian in origin, this rich, brown sauce is made from oysters and their brine, cooked with salt and soy sauce, and thickened with starches.

*sweet chilli* made from red chillies, sugar, garlic and vinegar. Has a comparatively mild heat.

*tomato* also known as ketchup or catsup; made from tomatoes, vinegar and spices.

*worcestershire* a thin, dark-brown spicy sauce.

**semolina** coarsely ground flour milled from durum wheat; the flour is used in making gnocchi, pasta and couscous.

**sour cream** thick, commercially-cultured sour cream with a minimum fat content of 35 per cent.

**soy milk** is rich creamy 'milk' extracted from soya beans that have been crushed in hot water and strained. It has a nutty flavour.

**silver beet** (swiss chard) also called, incorrectly, spinach; has fleshy stalks and large leaves and can be prepared as for spinach.

**spinach** also called english spinach and, incorrectly, silver beet. Baby spinach leaves are also available.

**star anise** a dried star-shaped pod with an astringent aniseed flavour.

**sugar**

*brown* a soft, finely granulated sugar retaining molasses for its characteristic colour and flavour.

*caster* also known as superfine or finely granulated table sugar.

*icing* also known as powdered sugar or confectioners' sugar; pulverised granulated sugar crushed with a small amount of cornflour.

*pure icing* also called powdered sugar or confectioners' sugar, but has no added cornflour.

**sultanas** also known as golden raisins; dried seedless white grapes.

**tofu** also known as bean curd, an off-white, custard-like product made from the 'milk' of crushed soy beans; comes fresh as soft or firm. Leftover fresh tofu can be refrigerated in water (changed daily) up to 4 days.

**vanilla**

*beans* dried, long, thin pod from a tropical golden orchid; the tiny black seeds inside the bean are used to impart a luscious vanilla flavour in baking and desserts.

*extract* made by pulping chopped vanilla beans with a mixture of alcohol and water. This gives a very strong solution, and only a couple of drops are needed to flavour most dishes.

**veal schnitzel** thinly sliced steak available plain (uncrumbed) or crumbed; we use plain schnitzel, sometimes called escalopes.

**zucchini** also known as courgette; small, pale- or dark-green, yellow or white vegetable belonging to the squash family.

# conversion chart

## measures

One Australian metric measuring cup holds approximately 250ml; one Australian metric tablespoon holds 20ml; one Australian metric teaspoon holds 5ml. The difference between one country's measuring cups and another's is within a two- or three-teaspoon variance, and will not affect your cooking results. North America, New Zealand and the United Kingdom use a 15ml tablespoon.

All cup and spoon measurements are level. The most accurate way of measuring dry ingredients is to weigh them. When measuring liquids, use a clear glass or plastic jug with the metric markings.

The imperial measurements used in these recipes are approximate only. Measurements for cake pans are approximate only. Using same-shaped cake pans of a similar size should not affect the outcome of your baking. We measure the inside top of the cake pan to determine sizes.

We use large eggs with an average weight of 60g.

## dry measures

| metric | imperial |
| --- | --- |
| 15g | ½oz |
| 30g | 1oz |
| 60g | 2oz |
| 90g | 3oz |
| 125g | 4oz (¼lb) |
| 155g | 5oz |
| 185g | 6oz |
| 220g | 7oz |
| 250g | 8oz (½lb) |
| 280g | 9oz |
| 315g | 10oz |
| 345g | 11oz |
| 375g | 12oz (¾lb) |
| 410g | 13oz |
| 440g | 14oz |
| 470g | 15oz |
| 500g | 16oz (1lb) |
| 750g | 24oz (1½lb) |
| 1kg | 32oz (2lb) |

## liquid measures

| metric | imperial |
| --- | --- |
| 30ml | 1 fluid oz |
| 60ml | 2 fluid oz |
| 100ml | 3 fluid oz |
| 125ml | 4 fluid oz |
| 150ml | 5 fluid oz |
| 190ml | 6 fluid oz |
| 250ml | 8 fluid oz |
| 300ml | 10 fluid oz |
| 500ml | 16 fluid oz |
| 600ml | 20 fluid oz |
| 1000ml (1 litre) | 1¾ pints |

## length measures

| metric | imperial |
| --- | --- |
| 3mm | ⅛in |
| 6mm | ¼in |
| 1cm | ½in |
| 2cm | ¾in |
| 2.5cm | 1in |
| 5cm | 2in |
| 6cm | 2½in |
| 8cm | 3in |
| 10cm | 4in |
| 13cm | 5in |
| 15cm | 6in |
| 18cm | 7in |
| 20cm | 8in |
| 22cm | 9in |
| 25cm | 10in |
| 28cm | 11in |
| 30cm | 12in (1ft) |

## oven temperatures

The oven temperatures in this book are for conventional ovens.
If you have a fan-forced oven, decrease the temperature by 10-20 degrees.

| | °C (CELSIUS) | °F (FAHRENHEIT) |
| --- | --- | --- |
| Very slow | 120 | 250 |
| Slow | 150 | 300 |
| Moderately slow | 160 | 325 |
| Moderate | 180 | 350 |
| Moderately hot | 200 | 400 |
| Hot | 220 | 425 |
| Very hot | 240 | 475 |

# index

# 3-5 years

# purées & mashes